INTERNATIONAL ADOPTION

Sensitive Advice
for
Prospective Parents

Jean Knoll and Mary-Kate Murphy

CHICAGO
REVIEW
PRESS

Library of Congress Cataloging-in-Publication Data

Knoll, Jean.
    International adoption : sensitive advice for prospective parents/
Jean Knoll and Mary-Kate Murphy.—1st ed.
    p.   cm.
    Includes index.
    ISBN 1-55652-211-8 : $12.95
    1. Intercountry adoption—United States.   I. Murphy, Mary-Kate,
1955- II. Title.
HV875.55.K63   1993
362.7'34'0973—dc20   93-41422
                                                      CIP

Published by Chicago Review Press, Incorporated
814 North Franklin Street, Chicago, Illinois 60610

Printed in the United States of America

ISBN: 1-55652-211- 8

1 2 3 4 5

To Maria, the Abuelita,
Charo, and most of all, to
Jessie, who together
made us a family.

—JK

~

To Peter, Matt, and Cristina
and to Elva
this book is lovingly dedicated

—KM

Contents

Preface

"Keep in mind always the present you are constructing. It should be the future you want."
—Alice Walker

Sensitive advice is what anyone looks for at the beginning of a venture that involves a longed-for goal, lots of hope, and little experience. Of course we look for straight information, but we'd like it to come with a little empathy, with some recognition of the emotional journey we may already have been on. And if advice comes from someone who has already taken the journey, perhaps it is that much more sensitive.

When we were asked to write a guide to international adoption two years ago, our reaction was one of delight—and uncertainty. Of course we wanted to tell the story of our daughters' adoptions, like any proud parents. Yet simply telling a story doesn't begin to explain the complicated workings of intercountry adoption ("international" and "intercountry" are used interchangably throughout this book, and mean the same thing). On the other hand, creating a book dense with document requirements, immigration law, steps toward an adoption decree, homestudy guides, and lists of travel items filled us with misgivings. Was that really the kind of book we felt prospective parents would want to read, or that we ourselves might have looked for at the beginning of our adoption ventures? Neither of us thought so. What we remembered needing in our early exploration of adoption was, truly, a little sensitive advice. The task, then, was to organize our book to accurately provide both an emotional as well as a factual context within which to explain intercountry adoption.

Luckily, the structure of the book was naturally suggested by the journals that Jean Knoll kept throughout the adoption process she experienced. The second element of the book—the "voices" of other adoptive parents—seemed a good way to reflect more accurately the many paths an international adoption might take, and were included in recognition of the fact that hard decisions involved in adoption are made more easily when others personally sit down and tell of their experiences and concerns. Even with the growing amount of information available today about adoption, there are people who still have very little personal contact with adoptive parents before they actually adopt.

The third element of the book, "commentaries," is Mary-Kate Murphy's primary contribution. Providing background for Jean's journals was important. A place was needed to tie sections of her journals together and explain parts of the adoption process and the current adoption scene. We added an appendix of resources for you, who we hope will be spurred on by reading our three-part treatment of the subject of intercountry adoption.

Jean's story, the backbone of this book, is a unique and contemplative journey. But we must stress that it is in no way meant to represent the experience of every family's intercountry adoption, nor is it the last word on all details involved in adoption. Though we've made every attempt to update all information, we must warn that since the international adoption scene changes rapidly, the best source of up-to-date information is your adoption agency and/or attorney. Parents recently returned from the country from which you hope to adopt are equally valuable resources, as are the many organizations and other references listed in our resources chapter.

A word about the voices of adoptive parents. Many absorbing hours were spent talking with parents about their intercountry adoption experiences, and it never failed to amaze us how different one story was from the other, yet how similar the emotional content of those stories was. In some cases, though, experiences were still so new or so deeply felt that parents were more comfortable speaking anonymously. In order to protect their privacy, some identifying details of some stories have been changed, and families' names do not appear with their narratives. Though we can't thank each individually, we're truly grateful for the gift of time and interest on the part of those parents who assisted with this manuscript.

Adoption is a lifelong series of discoveries about you, your child, and the world you inhabit. Starting that process of discovery even before your child arrives is the best investment you can make in the future of your family. It's only by thoughtful awareness of all the issues involved that adoptions can be not just successfully completed but deliberately, firmly, and lovingly established even before a child joins the family. If this book can be part of that process of discovery, our goal will be realized.

Jean Knoll
Mary-Kate Murphy

Introduction

Mary-Kate

There are times when I step outside myself and puzzle for a moment over the way life has turned out. Lots of adoptive parents must do this when they contemplate what life was like before they adopted and what life might have been had they not been joined to the child who is now theirs. Truly, and sometimes against all odds, adoption brings people together—and not just parents and children. I was fortunate that through the adoption of my daughter Jean Knoll and I became friends.

We met the night before I left South America to start my journey home to my husband Peter and son Matt after six weeks of waiting for my daughter Cristina's adoption to be completed. I had been told by my adoption coordinator that another adoptive parent would be arriving at the hotel that evening: a university professor from Chicago who was well traveled and spoke several languages. She was a single woman who had now (effortlessly, I was sure) made the decision to adopt. To me, who until several weeks earlier had never spoken Spanish or been any further south than Richmond, Virginia, this sounded like someone of great experience, confidence, and organization.

So you can imagine my surprise that evening when I opened the door to her hotel room. Inside was an uproar of luggage and boxes in piles all over the floor. On the bed in the midst of all this chaos sat Jean, looking . . . well, a little dazed, clearly overwhelmed, and not very worldly at all. She looked up, smiled a wobbly smile, and asked uncertainly "Do you know how to fix a bottle of baby formula?" So much for effortless sophistication. At that moment, I realized with relief that Jean, like me, was simply a new mother.

It was her immediate sense of trust, of establishing a temporary family out of the people who surrounded her, that was Jean's true "worldly" experience, and that quality served her well throughout the adoption of her daughter Jessie. Though I left after spending barely a day with her, I saw that her ability to ask for and give friendship was already creating a warm, familial circle full of instant aunts and uncles for herself and her little one. I was sorry to have to leave behind that sense of community and the new friend who seemed to fall into it so naturally. We vowed we would stay in touch and we have, sharing a mutual fascination for the subject of adoption and delight in our children. Our friendship is a good example of the fast bond that is often established between so many adoptive families who find themselves together during the often difficult experience of caring for a small child in a foreign country.

Jean's story is familiar to many of those parents. After all, thousands of Americans over the last decade have chosen to form their families by traveling to a foreign country, risking the unknowns of cost, bureaucracy, and uncertain outcome in order to fulfill their dream of a child. But Jean's story is different, too, in that she is single. In a trend first observed in the mid-1970s, a growing number of people have asserted their ability to parent in the absence of a mate by using adoption to form their families. Most single parents would agree that this decision is not made lightly, and that a certain amount of self-examination, inner strength, and self-belief is essential. These qualities don't appear out of nowhere, however, and aren't always intact during the adoption process. Jean used her journal as a safe place to record the exterior and interior journey she takes in developing these qualities, instinctively realizing that the power of fear and doubt is often reduced by writing it all down. And a journal is completely nonjudgmental about fears and doubts. During the difficult times she writes about, I sometimes get the feeling that Jean's journal is her most supportive and understanding confidant, a lesson from which both single and married people can learn. In fact, I'm struck by how often the emotions she expresses throughout her story matched my own, as I remember the unfolding of our daughter's adoption. Single or married, first- or second-time parents, we're all the same: adoptive parents trying to figure out this intensely emotional time in our lives.

Susan Cox of Holt International Children's Services (an adoption agency and relief organization), herself an adoptee, has said about adoption that "it's hard to feel good about where you are if you don't feel good about where you've been." She's talking about adopted children, about the importance of having a strong and positive view of their birth history; but I find this phrase can also apply to adoptive parents. It's a lot easier to see where you've been along the way to adoption when you use a journal, as Jean did. By keeping a record of events and emotions, parents get a sense of their own Life Before, of how they thought and felt and were before adopting and throughout the process. In a retrospective sense, a journal is a road map of specific decisions made on a journey, and of all the unique twists and turns that brought that parent to exactly the right child. It can help validate a belief in "shared fate": the conviction that those particular parents or parent and that particular child were meant to belong together. Along the way, the specific decisions of all parties—birthparents, caretakers, adoption workers, adoptive parents, and sometimes adoptees themselves—serve only to bring child and parent together.

There's no doubt in my mind that Jean and Jessie do belong together. By simply recording their adoption story, Jean has clearly ensured that the uniqueness of her family and the history of its formation is very special. If you are thinking of adopting, Jean and I can't urge you enough to document your own uniqueness through a journal. It will become a priceless record for you and your child in years to come.

Introduction

Jean

Late in the spring of 1988, I began what was to be the greatest journey of my life, to adopt a child internationally. The actual travel to South America, which I expected and looked forward to, was a great adventure; I had wanted to visit the Amazon rain forest since I was a little girl. Yet, the larger part of this journey, and the one I was perhaps least prepared for, was an interior one during which I confronted and came to terms with parts of my soul and heart I had never fully examined before.

That interior journey began when I realized the decision to adopt internationally meant giving up the idea that I would ever again have a "family" in the conventional sense of the word. No loving husband and would-be father joined me in this effort. No parents waited in the wings as supportive grandparents-to-be. And perhaps most difficult of all, it meant setting aside the idea of bearing my own biological children, temporarily perhaps but probably forever. Whatever might happen in the future, I will now never have a family where all the children look alike, and all of them look like me. Gradually, I came to understand that this has implications not only for where I will live and who will call me friend or lover; it also touches some of my own deepest and most carefully rationalized anxieties about genetic background and skin color.

Then, I had to examine what really motivated me to adopt. While many people have seen this as some sort of humanitarian gesture on my part, humanitarianism is by itself an unrealistic motive for adopting a child. Noble motives, like everything else, are hard to sustain day by day. In the end, I have had to acknowledge without shame that while I may indeed have helped someone else, this adoption is for the most part one of the most selfish things I have ever done. The delight I take each day in my beautiful daughter, as she grows into the person she is meant to be, is the greatest gift I have ever given myself.

And finally, I had to acknowledge that I would be tied forever to another country and another people if I am to help Jessie understand and respect who she is, where she comes from, and how she came to me. That tie has meant enormous changes in my life. At home we speak as much Spanish as English now. There is no cheating when we are tired or preoccupied; Tina, whose family has joined ours to help with child care, knows no English. It has meant the introduction of foods, customs, and holidays I never knew about before, and the invention of one very private celebration, "Gotcha Day," the anniversary of the day I first met Jessie. And most importantly, I am tied now to Peru through the biological family who gave my daughter life, through the friends who constituted our Peruvian "family" during my month-long stay there, and to the thousands of children who are born, live, and die in the poverty of Peruvian *barrios*, among whom Jessie would have been one.

When I was asked to write a book about my international adoption experience, I knew there was only one person with whom I wanted to write it: Mary-Kate Murphy. I knew that Katie, through her own adoption experience as well as her work with RESOLVE, an organization supporting the many families who cannot have biological children, would bring a far broader perspective than I to this intensely personal experience. Of all the people I knew, Katie would be able to set my own experience within the context of many others.

I met Katie in the chaos and confusion of my first hour of motherhood. In one of those rare moments in life, I remember knowing immediately that we were already friends. Katie and her daughter Cristina were to leave Iquitos the following day, but it was typical of Katie that she took the time yet that morning to walk me around town and show me the places and people that had become special to her. The last I saw of Katie and Cristina in Peru, they were sitting in the back of a broken-down van in the steaming jungle noon hour, waiting for the driver to tear himself away from a soccer game on the television to drive them to the airport. Cristina had already been touched by Katie's spirit (and Peter's, and Matt's, as I was to learn later): despite the discomfort and confusion, she wore a brave smile and waved furiously at the people they were leaving behind. When Jessie and I saw them again, the snow lay deep on the Illinois prairie. Halfway around the world the scene had changed and the girls were bigger, but nothing else was different. Katie and I were, as we have always been, old friends.

These journals then are the story of my journey, from my old life to my new one. Neither Katie nor I have formal expertise in social work, and certainly none in international adoption. Instead, what has guided me as I edited over two years of personal journals were three things. First, I hope that my experiences can be of some help to other people who have embarked on the long and often frustrating international adoption process, or are considering undertaking it. Though my journals remind me of how difficult it sometimes was, I hope this story will give them faith in happy endings. Second, I want to acknowledge the extraordinary love and support, past and present, of so many people who shared with me the ups and downs that led us all finally to my daughter's homecoming. And most of all, I wrote these journals for Jessie, so that she will have some understanding of what her coming has meant to me and of how, in turning my life upside down, she has somehow set it right.

Uncertain Beginnings

voices

It wasn't the decision to adopt that was such a big deal; it was the decision to have children. My husband and I had been together for ten years, and we cherished that time together. The idea of children was a brave new world for us. Making that initial decision was a struggle. But we finally decided that we did want kids; and as luck would have it, we discovered after a time with no result that we were infertile.

I know for some people infertility is a long, hard struggle. And for us it was at times anguishing. But actually, it was quick. I think we had a sense of humor about it, and we knew we didn't want it to go on and on. Not too long into the process we quickly decided that adoption was probably our solution. **(DE)**

I decided on adoption after I had been a foster parent for a year. I had worked with a fifteen-year-old in the local youth center and decided to apply for a foster care license when he was due to be released and would be needing a home. I figured if I could handle a teen, I could probably handle a young child.

Parts of the foster care experience were hard. But there were some really good things about it, and the good points for me were all about parenting. Billy lived with me for nine months. And I often say that I probably wouldn't have had Luba if I hadn't had Billy. **(LM)**

We decided two and a half years ago to have a second child. We wanted a larger family. But I was forty-four, my wife was thirty-nine, we'd had some problems having a biological child, and my wife hadn't particularly enjoyed childbirth. Also, philosophically I'm a believer in "one per couple." So for several reasons we decided that adoption would be best. As for the decision to go intercountry, . . . domestic adoptions seemed fraught with pitfalls, healthwise and legally. And I guess you could say that this kind of adoption makes a statement about our lives, our kind of "unitarian" belief in "one world, one people."

(BS)

No one could have been more astounded than I that I wanted a child. At the age of forty-three, I had never really longed to get married or have children. But somehow, the desire for a child kept growing, and I accepted it. The desire made me stick my little toe in the door. And slowly, one toe at a time, I found myself getting into the process. I nosed around; I nibbled at adoption agencies.

I was single when I started thinking about adoption, and I still am. I did consider domestic adoption for a short time, but the few domestic adoption agencies that would deal with single people said that in all likelihood I would get bumped by couples who were also waiting. I didn't want to set myself up for such disappointment, so I started looking at international adoption, which was less restrictive. It was frustrating to find out that other countries were more accepting of single adoptive parents than my own was!

What really convinced me at last to go ahead and get a homestudy done was being at one of the public meetings that agencies hold where international adoptive families come to talk about their experiences. I was so taken with the kids—they were all so happy, so rambunctious, so out there. Kids from everywhere in the world. Well, that clinched it. It seemed so right; I really felt after being at that meeting that adoption needed to happen for me.

I had concerns about adoption at the beginning, like everyone else. But here's something that helped during the process. My social worker, during the group homestudy process I went through, told us that it's important to get your negative ideas and worries out now. For example, do you worry that your baby might be ugly? I was horrified to hear that, because she was voicing exactly what I had secretly been thinking! She then told this story: She was present when an adoptive father saw a picture of his new child for the first time. "I have to say," the social worker told us, "that this baby was not very ... good looking, and I was worried. The adoptive parent looked at the photo and said, 'This is our baby? This is him? Boy, this baby's ugly.' Then he paused a moment and said with a smile, 'Guess I'll have to get used to it!'" I think the lesson in this story is don't shut off the conflicting and difficult feelings. Don't keep them secret. Because in acknowledging them, they lose their power. Secrets are powerful. **(PR)**

When a friend called recently to tell me she was pregnant with a third child and that she wasn't happy about it, it made me angry. You're upset over having a biological child, I think. Well, my husband and I have been going through hell. We're in the midst of an adoption situation that's taken months because of court shutdowns and lost paperwork. Our daughter has been in foster care all this time, and there's nothing we can do. You're upset? You at least have a choice about this. We have no choice about how we become parents. **(WK)**

When we decided to adopt internationally, I didn't know a soul who had done so—or even adopted. Anyone I did hear of who adopted from another country had adopted from Korea. We didn't realize there were other countries. So we assumed we'd be dealing with Korea. As it was, we heard that Korea was about to close its doors to adoption indefinitely (that was 1989; it did reopen the process some-time after). We had to search for an alternative. We looked at South American adoptions and decided on Colombia, because at that time the adoption process was completed pretty much before you arrived in the country and the stay was one week long. We couldn't afford to do it any other way.

My mother was not supportive of our decision to pursue interna-tional adoption. Couldn't you try harder? Try other doctors? How dark would this child be? It was fear of the unknown, really. It hurt to hear her be so negative. With that kind of reaction you have two choices: you can back down, or you can stand up and say, it's my life, my baby. If you can't accept it, it's your loss. Eventually and slowly, she did come around. In fact, she was at the airport waiting for us when we arrived home!

(MD)

I had been thinking about adoption for a while. About three years ago I finally said, Why not? I felt that fatherhood was eventually in the cards for me, that I would be a good father. I had been a Big Brother, a summer camp counselor, I had younger siblings . . . I like kids. I'm comfortable around them.

The idea of an intercountry adoption seemed self-evident to me. The idea had a spiritual quality for me. It wasn't because I was anxious to give some underprivileged child the benefits of American life. It just somehow felt right for me.

I never reached a point where I said NOW I'm ready. I just got started. I kept thinking, am I prepared for this? But I've never been really fully prepared for anything in my life. You know, you prepare yourself as best you can for all events, but you're never ever completely together at the time things happen. And that aspect of advancing into the unknown was exciting. **(KB)**

How did I decide to do this? Well, I'm one of those single forty-year-olds—forty-four, actually. The adoption system isn't much interested in us or in the nurturing skills we have. After calling around to a few adoption programs, I got to feeling that I'd probably missed the boat.

I met a couple who told me that they were off to China to adopt. Oh, how I'd love to be able to do that, I said. Well, you can, they said. You're actually almost old enough (at that time the Wuhan, China, program asked that singles be forty-five and older).

That was amazing to hear. It was great to have my age validated! There *was* a belief that I could love and take care of a child just as well as someone who is younger. I think the age requirement is indicative of the Chinese respect for age, a reflection of a society that honors their "elders." **(MEM)**

The actual infertility process was devastating—the monthly roller coaster, the tests, giving shots every night. But considering what we eventually went through . . . infertility was nothing! We were just getting ready for the really hard stuff. Because, you see, my wife and I went through the pain of a miscarriage. Then we had several adoptions fall through. And then we had an unbelievably difficult time getting through an intercountry adoption. It was probably a good thing that we went through infertility treatment. Otherwise we wouldn't have had any prep work and probably would have cracked up!   **(FJ)**

I wish I had had the kind of answers I have now for people curious about our choice of adoption. When I hear someone ask if you can truly love a child who isn't "your own," I say, look at the most time-honored and respected relationship our society has: marriage. It's the joining of two unrelated people—and the more unrelated, the better! That's easy for everyone to understand. Why should adoption be any different?

I tell you, breaking out of those molds is the challenge.   **(PM)**

Jean's Journal

July 20, 1988

Dear Jessie

(or maybe Sam . . . I think that I would like for you to be a Jessie, but who can tell what will happen? Who could imagine I would get to this point?),

I made the first phone calls to adoption agencies a few weeks ago. Since then, I've gathered stacks of papers and gone to informational meetings at what seem like a hundred agencies (though it was probably only five or six). I've seen a lawyer about how people arrange private adoptions. I've bought and read a dozen books. I have even gone to a single parents' support group, just to see what single parenting looks like. Now, tonight, I am starting this journal to my unknown daughter or son so that, if you ever do come, you will have a record of it all; so that one day you'll know what this long and unusual process has been.

Of course, I want a record, too, of the hopes and despairs that come with deciding to pursue parenthood through adoption, and without a partner; a place to work out my fears and doubts and to celebrate and remember my joys. And I want this journal to be an act of faith, dear child, that you will come into my life after all. Whatever I do not know about you, coming from somewhere beyond this seemingly endless process of papers and interviews and self-assessment, of one thing I am absolutely certain: I love you already.

I realized earlier today that I've been thinking about this journal for days but hesitating to start it. Odd, to be writing to a child I have never seen and who may not even exist. Yet one day, if and when you read this, you'll know this was the first time in my whole life that I was ever . . .

your loving Mama

August 15

Dear Jessie or Sam,

I try to understand when this process really began. I know it was long before the June phone calls, and probably even before I was aware of it. I remember first thinking about adoption a couple of years after my divorce. I called some agencies then and bought a book or two, but I never got much further. I suppose I still hoped that I could do it the "regular" way, as the outcome of the love of two people. I thought the father of my children had come in the spring of 1987 when I, your stable, well-adjusted future mother, fell desperately in love with a man I hardly knew. As it gradually became clear that we would not after all marry, I had a miscarriage. The pregnancy could not have been more than a few weeks along, and I had no suspicion of it until I lost it. I mourned for the loss of the man and his promise for a long time. And then, as that pain gradually subsided, I found I still mourned for the child that might have been.

At first I thought about becoming pregnant again, this time intentionally, and I read books and took my temperature and tried to imagine what it would be like not to be able to see my feet. For now though, I've decided not to try to become a biological parent. I suppose partly I fear what people (whoever "they" are) would say; I know people like my mother and father would probably never understand or approve. And partly, I can't imagine telling you one day about a father who would have been either someone I didn't love well enough to marry or some numbered test tube in a sperm bank. How could I conceive a child that way, I find myself asking, in a world where thousands of children already born die from hunger and want?

And if the truth be known, pregnancy doesn't look like much fun even under the best of circumstances, and becoming pregnant as I face my fortieth birthday isn't exactly the best of circumstances. I know that it takes time to recover from pregnancy and delivery, time during which I'd need someone (many someones probably) to be with me and the child I'd bear. With both my parents dead (and even if they were still alive), whom could I ask? Mind you, in spite of all these concerns, I'm not the most patient person in the world. If this adoption process looks as though it will take forever (which in my mind just now means much over a year), or if it appears that the only child I can adopt has "special needs" (a tactful term for the physically or mentally handicapped child who, it seems to me, needs *two* parents even more than most children), you may well come from my own body after all.

At least for now, I pursue the possibility of adoption. I have spoken to a very good attorney who works with the Episcopal Diocese of Chicago; the bishop says this attorney will give me good and ethical advice. What he tells me is not very encouraging. Unless I can find a pregnant woman who does not feel that she wants her child to have two parents, or who cannot find a suitable couple among the thousands who are trying, and a woman who can be convinced of my overwhelming virtue as a single parent, I will wait a long time . . . perhaps forever.

Others tell me I should try the want ads in selected areas. A student of mine who works in the Hispanic *barrio* in Chicago tells me how many children are born in that community who cannot be properly cared for. She took me for a walk through Pilsen the other day . . . so much poverty, and yet such apparent attachment of mothers to their children. How does one write in a few sentences the words to alter that? "Professor mother with more than enough of everything, especially love, wishes to share her life with a baby. Se habla español . . . "

I have also begun to work with an agency near Chicago that has some history of working with unmarried women who wish to adopt. I have told them I want a healthy infant, as close to new-born as possible. I will probably only do this once, and I'd like to experience as much of the entire process of your life as I can. They all say that I will need to adopt internationally, and they have given me a list of countries in Central and South America that will work with single parents. They have also given me more stacks of papers to fill out. Two sixteen-year-olds can make a baby in the back seat of a Chevy, but I have to get my house appraised.

I look at the list of countries: Ecuador, Peru, Paraguay, Guatemala . . . I need a map to be sure of exactly where they are. I realize suddenly, sitting here in my study with my degrees hanging on the wall, that I am abysmally ignorant about the part of the world from which you may come. How does one select among them? Prices, or what are more genteelly described as "country fees"? Length of waiting lists? Residency requirements? In Peru, the time to locate a child seems quite short, but the adoptive parent(s) must stay for six weeks or more—not a very good idea for a single mother who can afford only limited time away from her job. In Mexico, the same parent must stay only two days. I add to my reading list, which has recently come to include Dr. Spock and Dr. Brazelton, Fodor's. If I am to have a child from one of these countries, I had better at least find out where they are.

August 18

Dear Jessie or Sam,

They say it's important that my child knows that her or his biological mother was treated fairly, by me and by the process that leads her to me. I am shocked at how tempted I am, out of eagerness, to use my education and position in the community if they would speed this process along. In the end I know I couldn't live with that. More than that, I know I could never face you with it. That's part of what troubles me a little about the whole adoption process, wherever it occurs and however it is played out. In the end, though it is certainly about love, it is also about money and position, about those who have them and those who don't. The poor are its victims as well as its beneficiaries. Already I am wondering how I will answer, "Why did my birthmother give me to you?"

I am worried about another question too: "Where is my daddy?" For a long time I worried that all I could give you was half a family; that I would be using you to satisfy my own longings for a child instead of your needs for the two-parent family this society holds as ideal, however rare it is becoming in fact. But my friend Peggy, who has taught me so much about love, says that I'm not half of anything, and that if I don't stop this half business, she'll be mad. If I can wish for you anything already, I wish that one day you will have a friend like Peggy.

There is, so far at least, no adoptive father on the horizon, just a vast array of volunteer relatives. I am surprised by their unhesitating support of this idea. Lonnie and Naomi will be your "grandparents." Naomi has always wanted to knit all those sweet little things for babies, and she would do for a child of mine much of what my own mother would have done. My sister has already bought "a few" stuffed animals, the shelves groaning under their weight; Steve and Betty are looking for a stroller; Wong and Aiko will get us Pampers at a discount. A truly international family, this: black grandparents, Asian and Anglo godparents, and *gringa* mother and auntie. I have begun to realize that you and I have an incredible luxury here: the opportunity to select our own "relatives." It won't be the family I grew up in, but in some ways it may be an even stronger one because we are all so willingly a part of it. I wonder how old you will be before you recognize that most other families are not such a Rainbow Coalition, drawn together by love for a child.

I also wonder how old you will be before you realize our skin color is not the same. I wonder how long it will be before others comment on it. I have thought long and hard about whether I, a white woman, could successfully adopt and raise a black child, although the laws in this state would make that very difficult. I talked about it with Naomi and Lonnie, and especially with Naomi, who is so fair that one does not always recognize her as a black person. She told me with great sadness about her experience of being "too light to be black and too dark to be white." What issues would a black child face in white America that I have no experience of? How could I, a white mother, help a black teenager weather the storms of adolescence without having been there myself? I could do it as well as any white parent could, I suppose, but I wonder if that is enough. At least a child of Hispanic descent comes from a cultural heritage I have studied and visited, a language I can stumble around in. Enough, I suppose, to give me some sense that I could raise a Hispanic child with awareness of and respect for the land where she or he was born.

But who am I kidding? This is a racist culture, in a racist world. And I suspect that we will learn some things about it, through our experience together, that we might prefer not to know at all.

September 5

Dear Jessie or Sam,

The weather of this unbearable summer has finally turned cool, and with it I finish the initial steps of adoption. I am collecting the last of the first phase of paperwork—my physical exam, my police clearance, my bank statements—this week. In a week or two Julie, the social worker who has been doing the homestudy to license me as a foster parent (which is required if I wish to bring a child here from another state, let alone another country), will come for a "home visit." She will be sure that there is enough room here for a child, that the plumbing works, and that the place is (relatively speaking, at least) clean. And then, I wait. I don't think much right now about becoming pregnant. I wonder if one can do both at the same time. I can't imagine having the emotional stamina to add to all of this the anxiety of fertility tests.

All summer long there has been construction in this old house: a new laundry room for little clothes, a sink in your nursery, a reopened fireplace in my bedroom. I have this vision of sitting in a rocker by that fireplace, with you wrapped in a soft blanket having your 2:00 A.M. bottle. Experienced parents laugh out loud at this; they say it is the fantasy of a woman who has never faced a 2:00 A.M. feeding.

I've even begun to think about changing jobs. All my life I've wanted the career I finally have. Now, even before you are here, it is surprisingly easy to imagine setting it aside to stay home with you, watching you grow and change and learn. Not that I have a choice as a single parent. Perhaps that will minimize at least the guilt so many mothers feel when they go back to work after having a child. There aren't really any alternatives for me, though I've begun to wish there were.

I've also begun to realize for the first time how difficult it will be to cut back from my sixty-hour work weeks—hard because my colleagues and my students have come to expect that much work and availability from me, and hard because at some level I've come to expect it of myself as well. I wonder if it wouldn't be easier to start again somewhere else, in a job that has meant less to me in the past, has been less of a refuge for me, and less of a cause. Already I realize how precious our time together will be, and how brief. Remarkable, isn't it, how much a woman can invest in a career and how easily she can be tempted to put it all aside for the sake of her children?

I spent today playing with my godchildren, and I saw again how wonderful and how difficult being a parent is. I also realized how grounded I feel when I'm with them, how orderly the universe seems and how in touch with life they bring me. And yet, I am also afraid of how this will all work out. My stomach churns with my own version of morning sickness as my first trimester in the adoption process ends. What will you be like? Will you like me? Will we somehow manage the logistics of child care and job and personal life, and still have something left over, that elusive "quality time" the books talk about, for each other? Will I, at my age, be able to manage the fatigue and the lifting? I remember a friend who had her first child at the age of thirty-nine who said that she now understood why God made women most fertile in their twenties.

I've learned, God knows, how to cope for myself after all these postmarriage years and the death of my parents. But you are another person, whose life will be inexorably changed by all I choose to cope with. How will I know how to do it right?

September 25

Dear Jessie

(Yes, you are now almost surely Jessie—one advantage of adoption over biology is that one can sometimes request a gender. Oddly, they say that in South America it takes more time to locate infant girls than infant boys—I wonder why),

In international adoption, parents often work with two agencies, each with their own requirements, paperwork, and fees. A domestic agency does the homestudy and licenses adoptive parents, and an international agency works with on-site contacts in foreign countries to locate children appropriate for adoption. I picked the first agency with great care, visiting their information sessions, meeting their social workers, and talking to parents who have worked with them before. It was because of my wonderful social worker, Julie, and her support of me as I become a single parent that I selected my local agency.

Finding an international agency has been much more a shot in the dark. Local agencies have relationships with foreign adoption agencies, so adoptive parents usually start there. Then we go by the recommendations of others, as I did in selecting the foreign adoption agency in Michigan that I've decided to try. They seem honest, although such agencies are loosely regulated at best, at least if a call to the state agency in Michigan that keeps track of such places is any example. I like the people at the agency that I talk to on the phone. They say their lists are shorter than other agencies because they are newer, but consequently they also have less of a track record and fewer names of other families with whom they have worked. In the end, the shortness of their waiting list probably has persuaded me more than anything else. Odd though, to have someone look for my daughter without ever having met them.

Now that I have decided on an agency, how do I select among the various countries in which they operate? The waiting time before you can be located is what I thought of first, and of course the fees. Next, how long must I stay in the country of origin? Parents do not always have to go, I realize; children from India, for example, arrive several times a week at O'Hare Airport, in the arms of escorts who simply present them to their new families. But I would like to see where you were born, to know more about the culture, perhaps even to meet your birthfamily so I can tell you about them. For some countries, adoptive parents make two trips: one to take initial custody and begin the adoption process, and a second, after varying periods of time, to conclude the adoption and bring the child home. I think it would almost kill me to bond with you and then to leave, knowing that even in the best of foster care, you are growing up rapidly without me. So I look for a country with only one required visit of a reasonable length of time. And finally, I want to finalize the adoption in the country of origin and before I travel back to the States. In some countries, one takes provisional custody of a child and then completes the adoption process at home. But it would seem risky to take a child for whom I do not have final, legal responsibility out of a foreign country.

Could someone revoke my custody at the airport? Or even after I'm home? No, absolutely, I will adopt only where I can finalize in the country of origin. Given my criteria, the agency recommends Paraguay.

Where on God's green earth is Paraguay?

September 30

Dear Jessie,

I think adoption has more similarities to pregnancy than people know. A month or two ago, when I was still filling out papers, a baby was unreal to me. As certain as I was, and am, that this is the right decision, how could I, for heaven's sake, have a baby in my life? I, who don't know a diaper rash from prickly heat. I, who sometimes leave for work before sunrise and often don't return till well after dark? Until earlier this week, you were still in many ways an abstraction.

Then, a few days ago (on September 27), the people in Michigan called to tell me that several babies were likely to be identified in Paraguay shortly. If I move quickly, they say, you might actually be here for Christmas—you might already even be born. Suddenly, I can imagine the feelings that pregnant women often think are gas as they move from the first to second trimester, feelings they soon realize are actually the flutter of life itself. Each step I take from now on brings me tangibly closer to the daughter I dream about at night. I always plant spring bulbs this time of year, but I know this fall that when they bloom for the first time you may well be here to see them. I think perhaps I should go out and buy more, to make a bouquet, an entire garden, to welcome you to this world.

As the process becomes more concrete, now I'm getting excited and nervous about the decision to travel to South America. I've traveled before, sometimes to exotic and far-off places, but always alone, worried only for myself and confident that nothing could happen to me that could not be resolved (or escaped) with my American Express card. The adoption agency's literature says to pack as if I were traveling with a baby; but what do babies need when they travel? And what will *you*, Jessie, need? What kind of formula? What size diapers, and how many? I am learning as I ask advice of my friends who are already mothers that they, too, can only guess. Not many people have traveled with young infants in foreign countries for weeks at a time. What do I do with no twenty-four-hour drugstore nearby?

Yesterday, I bravely tried to face down a few of the butterflies in my stomach. I went to a baby store, intent on buying toys and little clothes, sweet little dresses and blankets to wrap you up like the gift you will be to me. Instead, everything I've learned from being a godmother and an aunt (not very much, it turns out) deserted me at the door. Could I possibly be as lost and confused in South America as I was when I crossed that threshold and entered Babyland? The owner of the store, a gentle older man, came up and asked if he could help me. He took my elbow to give me support. And I blurted out, "I don't know what any of this is, or what it does, or how many I need, and I probably shouldn't be here anyway!" Out of the store I ran, to compose myself on the sidewalk. I can do this, I thought, breathing deeply. The professor in me can go back in there and at least buy a book.

My friends who are parents have told me: The first trimester is for disbelief. The second is for reading.

Uncertain Beginnings

commentary

For most people who eventually decide to adopt, disbelief sets in long before adoption feels like even a possibility. For some, the disbelief starts as they realize that conceiving isn't the easy biological miracle they assumed it would be. For others, it is the circumstances of their lives that cause disbelief. "Who could imagine I would get to this point?" Jean writes. It is a common cry of despair, and it's part of my past, too.

Like so many infertile people, I despaired often. Not even quitting my dead-end job and going back to school solved the infertility. Like 50 percent of all infertile women (according to the National Center for Health Statistics), I was already a parent; Peter and I had been lucky enough to conceive our son Matt in 1984. But several years later, it became obvious that we were facing problems trying to conceive a second child, and we began traveling a complex route of diagnoses and medications. Adoption was one idea we neatly sidestepped.

After four years of trying and failing, we reached a low point in our quest for a baby. We planned an evening out on the town for our seventh wedding anniversary, but as often happened during those gloomy years, we only made it halfway through dinner before the conversation turned to infertility. My tears began to flow. At the arrival of a classic happy couple and their brand-new infant at the next table, my feeling of defeat was final; we paid the bill, headed home, and had a furious argument that in the end made us fear both for our marriage and our sanity. How tired we were of infertility. The monthly disappointments, our son's questions, the thought of one more high-tech medical treatment—the eternal carrot on a stick—just made us more crazy. We were sick of being human pincushions and wanted only to get on with our family. Wearily, we knew that we finally had to leave biology behind: medical treatment could only keep us guessing at our chances for another child. Maybe adoption . . . maybe that was our answer. Adoption could complete our family. Infertility, we had come to see, could tear it apart.

The decision to explore the idea of adoption didn't instantly make things better. Throughout the fall of 1989, I seemed to cry continually. I knew that adoption would be a good solution for us, but I still couldn't stop crying about it. I secretly doubted that it could work. We went to an adoption information meeting, but seeing all those happy families gathered to tell their stories made me reach for another tissue. It was a frustrating time: we really wanted to get going on the "next step," but I honestly couldn't bring myself to feel good about it. I guessed I was mourning the biological child who would never be, but my grief seemed to go beyond that. I felt so sorry about . . . I just didn't know what.

It was through my good friend Betsy that I finally found the words to describe what I was feeling. One day, we were talking about her situation; she was a single woman who, despite a full and satisfying life, had not yet found the "man of her dreams." "Sometimes I feel so sad," she said. "Not because I never found the man of my dreams, or that I found true love and then lost it. It's not that simple. It's that I don't know anymore what I'm even looking for. I feel like I've lost something, but I'm not even sure it was ever there in the first place." It occurred to me that Betsy was describing the same feelings I had been having about giving up on pregnancy. It seemed odd that her grief sounded so much like mine, but after talking about it we realized that we were both struggling to let go not of someone but of the idea of something. We were saying good-bye to hopes and expectations that we had truly grown to love.

I found later that most adoptive parents share these feelings. And it was also a comfort to learn that we mourn the loss of not just one, but an actual series of expectations or ideas. Through a workshop presented by Patricia Irwin Johnston (later released in book form as *Adopting after Infertility*, Perspectives Press, 1992), I found a full explanation of what I was experiencing.

Actual losses, Irwin said, are difficult to come to terms with but aren't hard to identify. A miscarriage, the termination of a significant relationship, the failure of medical treatment to correct infertility, the death of a spouse—all concretely point to a lost opportunity to experience a pregnancy and, ultimately, to parent.

Perceived losses are harder to pinpoint but are just as painfully felt. First, there is a loss of control over our situation when we realize that we don't have the option, for whatever reason, to biologically produce a child on our own. The confusion and anger we feel causes the familiar cry, "This isn't what I thought my life would be like!" We have the same reaction as we discover just how complex the adoption process is and how much time, money, and effort can be spent on it. Obviously, the hard, "unnatural" decisions involved in adoption don't look anything like the "natural," wondrous process of pregnancy and birth. It's not uncommon to feel cheated—after all, a promised life experience has been taken away.

We also realize that we face the loss of our ability to produce a genetic bond that perpetuates a family line or joins us to our partner. Sorrow over this loss can be compounded by an overwhelming sense of guilt over our inability to fulfill our "responsibility" for providing a connection between past, present, and future. Related to that, the loss of a biological connection to a beloved partner can provoke a great feeling of grief over the "failure" to create such a visible expression of love.

As an aside, it's interesting to note that these particular issues don't create problems for some people. "I'm so grateful that my son has no genetic tie to me," as one adoptive parent put it. "You have no idea what a horrible health history my family has." Another parent has mused that adopting has somehow freed her from some fearful expectations. "I was really introverted and painfully shy growing up, especially as an adolescent. My outgoing, very social mother was always pushing me to `get more involved,' try out for the school play, work on the school newspaper—stuff that just wasn't me. One day I must have completely frustrated her because I remember her yelling that I was turning out just like my father's sister Margery, `like all the wilting wallflowers in that family!' That remark always stuck with me, to the point that I began to believe that any little girl born to me would be doomed to grow up as painfully as I did. So it was like a secret relief to find out that we couldn't conceive. Adoption freed me from all my expectations. Even if my daughter turns out to be really shy, at least I'll know that it wasn't my genes that made her that way!"

Finally, Johnston pointed out that infertile people mourn the loss of not just the short-term experience of conceiving and bearing a biological offspring, but the long-term experience of parenting. It was by realizing that the two—biological recreation and parenting—could be separate that had already sent Peter and me off on the path toward adoption. In our heads, we knew this was logical. But in the fall of 1989 as Betsy and I talked through our mutual sadness, I finally came to understand that a logical progression from stopping infertility treatment to starting the adoption process would not be possible unless I stopped for a while to say good-bye to the idea of a child I had grown to love so much—perhaps too much, as Peter and I watched that dream threaten our relationship and family life.

But my chances to parent were not gone; they had simply shifted. As I cried that fall, my despair began to change a little. Adoption began to seem more possible; it even began to feel more like a choice than something we were pushed into. I had my last appointment with our infertility specialist; we had resolved not to pursue conception and adoption simultaneously. As I drove away from the medical center, I started to cry again—at first in grief, and then more and more in relief. Lots of books had told me that there would be a point at which I'd know it was time to move on. At last I could believe I had reached that point.

Up until late 1989, we had made halfhearted attempts to find out more about adoption. At one point, Peter opened the yellow pages and called the agencies listed under "Adoptions." They sent us information and notices of meetings and forms to fill out. The papers and brochures hung around for a while, but eventually Peter filed them away in an unmarked folder in our file drawer. Ending our medical treatment had been a relief, but evidently it hadn't yet filled me with a sense of new direction.

I began to do some of my own "research." Tentatively, I started to mention the possibility of adoption to a few friends. Most people smiled and said some encouraging things but could offer little else; nobody knew any more about adoption than I did. When I finally got around to talking with the only adoptive parent I knew, she completely overwhelmed me with her reaction. "Well, of course you should adopt! I don't understand why you spent so long on that medical stuff, anyway. Get your name on a list with a couple of agencies. Do it tomorrow! Homestudies can take a long time."

I left the conversation feeling confused and indignant. What a thing to say! I fumed to myself. She has no idea how hard things have been! It takes time to make such big decisions . . . it's not that easy . . . I can't just jump right in . . . I don't do things that way . . . I haven't gotten comfortable with the idea yet . . . Besides, what does she mean, get on a list? Where? And this "homestudy" thing. What's that?

After I spent a while getting angry over the kick in the pants my friend had given me, I began to appreciate it. I felt astonished by the instant sense of immobility her remarks had provoked in me. It seemed that infertility treatment had left me with a sense of pessimism that was keeping me down; and that attitude, I now realized, was useless baggage. Enough! I began to feel my anger give way to an energy I hadn't had for a long time. Peter, who had been ready to start the adoption process for a while but had realized that I needed time, was more than happy to pull the adoption file out of our drawer. Now we were both in the same place, at the same time.

We started our search for information. First, we went back to the yellow pages list of adoption agencies. We read over everything they had sent us from our file folder and studied the agency applications and fee schedules. Next, we called around and found some adoptive parents to talk to and asked for their recommendations. We found we would have to work with some kind of agency to get the adoption process going, and eventually we narrowed our search to one whose director was actually willing to spend close to an hour on the telephone with me, patiently unraveling the complexities of adoption and quietly listening to my concerns.

The process does take some explanation. Adoptions, whether they are domestic (U.S. parents adopting U.S. children) or international (U.S. parents adopting children from other countries) can be of two varieties: agency or independent. Agency adoptions are arranged under the supervision of an adoption agency that traditionally takes applications from both prospective adoptive parents and birthparents, and administrates the process of matching up families and children. Birthparents relinquish custody of their children to an agency, giving it the legal responsibility to assign new parents to the child and to take care of all paperwork and legal arrangements. Custody is then transferred from the agency to the child's adoptive parents. This is the usual practice for domestic agency adoptions; for intercountry agency adoptions, the U.S. adoption agency works on the one hand with prospective adoptive parents and on the other with a foreign entity—a foreign orphanage, or private or governmental placement program. Acting as a crucial intermediary, the U.S. adoption agency provides oversight of the adoption process as it does in a domestic agency adoption.

Independent adoptions, also known as "private" or "identified," are arranged and legally contracted between birthparents and adoptive parents without the legal involvement of an adoption agency (some independent domestic adoptions are facilitated by adoption support agencies, or "nontraditional agencies" found throughout the country, that work with adopters to initiate adoption searches and help insure that birthparents have proper counseling and health care). No matter how independent adoptions are arranged, all must be completed with the assistance of a lawyer. Birthparents and adoptive parents in the United States find each other through many sources—doctors, ministers, lawyers, friends of friends, newspaper ads. Independent intercountry adoption, also done without the intervention of an adoption agency, can be arranged by contracting directly with a foreign lawyer or with an adoption coordinator (often someone with ties in both the United States and the foreign country) in conjunction with a foreign lawyer. Both coordinator and/or lawyer identify children and match them with prospective overseas parents. As in the case of some domestic independent adoptions, some intercountry independent adoptions can be facilitated by adoption support intermediaries—parent groups or individuals who provide adoption information and advise prospective parents in identifying foreign lawyers to work with on an adoption. Such intermediaries are usually found through parents who have adopted previously.

No matter what the type of adoption—domestic or intercountry, independent or agency—all prospective adoptive families must undergo the homestudy process before any adoption can take place. A homestudy is a document written by a social worker usually employed by a licensed agency. It presents a detailed analysis of the prospective adoptive parent or parents, typically based on a series of interviews and meetings and topped off by a visit to the future adoptive home. In an agency setting, homestudies are done after the prospective adopter fills out an initial application to the agency; matching of children and adoptive parents is not done until completion and approval of the homestudy. Prior to any independent adoption, an approved homestudy must also be in place, but it is the responsibility of the independent adopter to have a homestudy completed before identifying and taking custody of any child.

These days, traditional adoption agencies (those that service the entire adoptive triad—birthparents, child, and adoptive parents) are not the only places a prospective adoptive parent wishing to adopt independently can go to get a homestudy done. Adoption agencies have sprung up that service only the prospective adoptive parents: they perform homestudies and then refer adopters on to programs that locate infants or children living either in the United States or overseas who are waiting for homes. It was this kind of agency we settled on to help us adopt.

Several circumstances had caused us to choose this particular route. In the first place, we knew that our chances for doing a traditional, domestic agency adoption were slim. We were facing stiff competition: the Bureau of National Affairs estimates that each year close to two million couples and one million single people seek to adopt, a hefty reminder of both an ever-present infertility problem that affects one in twelve couples nationwide, and the growing realization of society in general and single people in particular that single people can and want to parent too. Traditional agencies, driven by these overwhelming numbers, place restrictions on candidates for adoption: preferred adopters are young, married couples without children. Next in line come families with children, and last of all come single people like Jean. Clearly, we were at a disadvantage with a domestic adoption agency.

Independent adoption, therefore, would be the route we would take. It also seemed the way to go because we were looking to adopt as young a child as possible; our son was getting older and we wanted to minimize the age difference between him and his new sister or brother. Domestic independent adoptions are usually infant placements. That seemed right. But we were uneasy about finding a baby through a newspaper ad, and we didn't know how long it might take. We knew some people were lucky and were able to make contact with birthparents fairly quickly, but that wasn't always the case. Would we have to wait another four years? After our struggle with infertility, we weren't sure we could face that.

Our adoption agency was one that, after completing a clients' homestudy, offered contacts with both domestic and intercountry adoption programs. The agency director wisely refused to promise a fast process for any program she recommended, but she did say that some adoptions that moved quickly were done overseas. Intercountry adoption, if we were willing to consider it, might be our best choice.

Like Jean, therefore, we found that many circumstances drove us to decide on international adoption. But we weren't disappointed by the prospect—in fact, we felt more drawn to possibilities further afield. Why? Maybe our reasons were altruistic: we were members of Amnesty International, the worldwide human rights organization, and we knew about the poverty and terrorism that endangers so many children of the Third World. Adoption could give us the opportunity to help just one. Maybe we saw a chance to explore: traveling to another country to adopt a child could be exciting; and we would have the benefit of incorporating another culture into our family. Maybe we were too impatient: we didn't want to wait for a domestic adoption, and we knew that there were many waiting children throughout Asia and Latin America.

Maybe we were scared. We knew that there were also many waiting black or biracial children here in the United States. But like Jean, we also knew that the culture of African Americans includes the onerous history of black and white relations in this country. We knew, too, of the opposition to transracial adoption by groups such as the National Association of Black Social Workers. We weren't sure we disagreed with their view that white parents are not equipped to handle the special problems of black identity and self-esteem. I feared that such difficult identity issues might end up disrupting our family; I feared that political issues of oppression, past and present, might end up entangled within our family structure. I feared that I might not be able to come to terms with my white guilt, and I didn't want to use adoption—and the child who would become my son or daughter—to try to heal that issue.

We decided to try to adopt a child from South America. Therefore, though our child would not be African American, he or she would certainly differ from us racially, at once and forever placing us in a different "category" in white America. We were destined to become a minority family: one that contained a member of a minority, and a family that, because of its mixed composition, would be unlike most American families. If this were something we could handle within the privacy and with the support of our immediate family and friends, we knew we would have few problems. But as we've since found out, simply taking the kids to the grocery store sometimes prompts people to remind us that we don't look like a normal American family. Often, the comments they feel compelled to make (usually when we're simply trying to hurry home to dinner) are gracious. Some you wouldn't believe.

"Oh . . . she's so brown" or "You went to Peru (or Korea or Colombia) to adopt? Don't you think we should be taking care of our own?" are good—and actual—examples of particularly bad comments. Is it simply thoughtlessness? Or is it prejudice? We live "in a racist culture, in a racist world," Jean says. I would dearly like to disbelieve her words. Yet I realize my children's future experiences will include encounters with people I can't always pull aside and attempt to "educate."

Educating others is one thing; educating myself is another. During our homestudy, my husband and I were urged to read and learn about all the issues involved in adoption, particularly the intercountry variety. At a daylong conference for adoptive families, we attended a workshop in which a panel of adoptive parents talked about the importance of self-esteem for children of color. Our neighbor Maureen was one of the speakers. "I have two sons from Colombia," she said. "And in our house, we talk a lot about melanin. Does everyone know what that is?" The word was vaguely familiar. "It's a substance in skin cells," she said. "If you have more melanin, you're darker. If you have less, you're lighter." Well, I thought, that's simple! That's all the explanation anyone should need to explain dark and light skin. My six-year-old can understand that, and so will his future sibling—as will our friends and neighbors and family. Anyone could understand that. Couldn't they? But as the rest of the panelists spoke about teaching their children pride in their cultures and color, and how important that pride was in the face of comments and taunts of classmates, it was clear that things weren't so simple. I saw that knowing about melanin is an easy answer to an enormously complex problem. Kids who ridicule others for their color can be taught the biology of skin in the classroom, but it wouldn't do away with the lessons those kids learn at home. How many children live with and listen to adults who left melanin far behind in their sixth- grade science class? Despite what those parents learned in school, American social issues have wiped out any memory.

That workshop nagged at me for days. Of course I knew what racism was. Like every liberal white American, it saddened me. But I had never been personally affected by it—until now. It was sobering to realize that I knew about, but didn't truly understand, the jump from skin color to racism; and that until this late date, I had never really wondered why. I had been basically untouched by it—but no longer. Before I might have to start explaining things to my son and future daughter, I felt I had to understand just a few more basics.

I searched out an older but fascinating source to help me. In his 1954 book *The Nature of Prejudice* Gordon Allport details the growth of prejudice and its development into racism. Allport notes that human beings often look for something that will make them feel more powerful over others. The easiest way to do this is to find something that's easy to recognize—like skin color. To strengthen this artificial advantage, power seekers choose to stick to their own kind, to socialize and live only with those of their own color. After a while, anyone who looks different on the outside appears to be different on the inside. That belief grows; soon, color appears to say something about intelligence or ability and begins to signify something evil or threatening.

When people of the same viewpoint group together, their collective strength gives them a feeling of superiority, and anybody who suggests that their prejudices might be based on false assumptions is subject to ridicule or anger—expressions of the fear of losing power. Children, as the most avid joiners of groups and the most vulnerable of group members, will do anything to establish their place and avoid alienation. Therefore, they take the most logical path: they mimic the viewpoints of their adult superiors. Racism is

established and flourishes within a suppressive and critical atmo-
sphere that is passed on within communities of people and through
generations.

Allport's explanations were dispassionate, but reassuring. I felt
my understanding about this new part of my life grow, and I felt
assured that understanding the roots of these issues would help me
help my children and their friends and family understand. However, I was discovering that uneasiness with the decision to adopt a
child of color can begin to appear even before the child is brought
home. "We've decided to adopt" was greeted by our families with
a hesitation that was quickly replaced with relief and excitement.
"We've decided to try intercountry adoption" provoked bewilder-
ment and uneasiness. "Are you sure that's really what you want?"
seemed to be the unspoken question. Among the adoptive parents
I've talked to, outright family disapproval of their adopted children
is rare, and for most families, like mine, there are definite and
ongoing positive adjustments in attitude. The unfortunate and
unwavering hostility of a family member can only be dealt with by
staying away. It's a shame, but it may change with time.

At least attitudes grow more positively through the fascination
so many people feel for different cultures. Families are excited and
enriched by this aspect of international adoption, and we were no
exception. Imagine my dismay, then, to find that information
about South America is not as available as I had expected. Just like
Jean, I ran right out to get Fodor's *South America* travel guide
when we firmly decided to try to adopt from that part of the world.
But beyond that, the frustrating search for better information
confused me. I noticed how relatively little news about South
American politics reached our local newspaper. I scouted in vain
for books about South American countries. Mostly, I found com-
pendiums that talked in general about "the people of South America," and then spent many pages describing the lives of the Spanish
conquistadors without mentioning the indigenous Indian populations with whom the Spanish mixed, and from whom most people
in South America are descended. Even looking at my world atlas
disturbed me, when I realized that eighteen maps covered the
continent of Europe, but only four were used to show Mexico,
Central America, the West Indies, and the continent of South
America combined. The atlas's introduction explained that less
space was devoted to some countries of the world if those countries

were of lesser relative importance. To whom? I wondered. Spanish is the second most-spoken language in the United States today, the legacy of millions of immigrants from all parts of Latin America. What would be more important to those people—a map of Puerto Rico (a one-inch-square insert on one of the atlas pages) or one of France (a full-page map, followed by two pages of description)? It seems the world has been shifting in past decades, but the tools we use to learn about society are still more "Eurocentric" than our nation actually is. I can't deny that money and power lie to a great extent in the hands of those of European descent, but we as a society can no longer teach that the rest of the world is therefore of lesser importance.

It means work to adopt a child of a different race and culture. It adds another dimension, above and beyond the issue of adoption, in becoming and maintaining a healthy family. Perhaps we were naively idealistic when we looked to another country for our second child, but in the end we felt that the choice was a challenge, one we wanted and could handle. Of course we expected struggles, but we also suspected that this adoption would ultimately bring us great happiness. "You make your choices and you take your chances," a good friend has always said. We could only hope that the choices we were fortunate enough to make would lead us to a birthmother who might take a chance with us.

Telephone Calls and Other Connections

voices

How did we find out about our child? The modern way, I guess—our agency left a message on the answering machine. We called back immediately—as soon as we got home from work. They said that a baby girl had been born, and after the weekend they would know if she might be the one for us. That weekend seemed to last forever. Finally, early the next week, they told us that the child—eventually our oldest daughter, Marisa—was available and we said yes. Yes!

I remember getting the Federal Express packet that contained the first pictures we had of her. I still have that envelope. It was delivered to me at work, and I rushed over to my husband's office so we could open it together. What a moment. There were photos of a tiny infant with a scrunched-up baby face. We couldn't find any other details in the picture, and all that was written on the back was "niña, dos dias" ("baby girl, two days old"). At that point all we knew was her birth date and that she was healthy. It was hard not knowing any more, but eventually we received lots more information and even more pictures before we traveled to meet her, thanks to our adoption coordinator. Those pictures helped us so much; we kind of watched her grow and really started feeling this connection to her. We put one picture in a frame and had it in our bedroom. That was one very important photograph. Especially since we didn't meet her until she was ten weeks old.

For the adoption of our second daughter, Lia, our agency was no longer facilitating Paraguayan adoptions. But through a friend who was fluent in Spanish, we were still in contact with our lawyer in Paraguay, who said she would keep her eye out for us. Politically, the country had gone through a lot—there had been a coup, and with all the upheaval the country stopped allowing international adoptions. We knew it was almost certain we wouldn't be able to adopt from Paraguay again, but our friend kept calling our lawyer occasionally. After a while we heard that adoptions might start up again in Paraguay, and we began to hope a little bit.

Well, one day our friend called to tell us she had been talking with our lawyer and had been waiting for some details to be worked out, but that finally she could tell us—we were the last to know!—that a baby had been born. It was June, and we were outside on the deck. I started screaming, "The baby! The baby's been born!" We went nuts. My husband and I were running around the yard, yelling like two crazy people . . . and there was Marisa, playing in the sand with a bucket and shovel, completely oblivious. I don't even think she heard us. **(DE)**

Learning about our son was actually a very straightforward affair. We were given an appointment with our adoption agency. They had a relationship with a Korean agency that would periodically send them "offerings" of several children for whom homes needed to be found. So our agency had a big file of children and information; you're given a picture and then you spend some time talking with the social worker. And then you're asked to make a decision. **(FEM)**

I spent much of 1992 pursuing an adoption in South America that eventually fell through. But in the spring of 1993, I received information from the Committee for Single Adoptive Families about an adoption agency in the Southwest that had been successful with Russian adoptions. My homestudy agency said they'd look into it for me, and to my amazement I found a message on my machine that evening saying that the agency had two referrals of Russian boys, aged five and seven, both cleared for adoption and living in orphanages. I called as soon as I could and asked for more information about the seven-year-old. What else can you tell me about him? Do you have any pictures available? No photos, they told me, but we do have a video. They express-mailed it to me. The next day, I found myself glued to the TV screen while this little boy recited a Russian epic poem from memory. It was quite a moment. I thought, "This is it. This is the perfect kid for me. And he's been waiting for me for seven years and I didn't know it!"

That was April. Three months later I was on the plane to Moscow.

(KR)

I met someone who had adopted from Honduras. She acted as my liaison, and got me in touch with her Honduran lawyer. But it turned out the lawyer wasn't trustworthy. After agreeing to work with him, I waited and waited, but heard nothing for three months. Then I got a letter from my contact, who told me the lawyer had recently been in the United States and had actually spent some time in my area. But he hadn't bothered to contact me. Oh, and by the way, my contact wrote, the lawyer was doubling his fee. I blew my stack. I told my contact that I would not work with this guy if he were going to pull this kind of stuff. When the lawyer heard about that—he fired me! So my only in-country contact was out the window, and I was right back to square one. How typical that is in international adoption: either you have the right contact—or you don't, in which case everything falls apart all at once. Luckily, though, I got the name of an independent adoption consultant in Atlanta. I called her. In the middle of our conversation, she asked if my paperwork was already in Honduras. I said it was. She said if everything was in order she was sure she could help me, and I might even hear from her very shortly. Based on my past experience, I thought, well, that probably means a month or two. Well, in three days she called and said, I think we have a baby—two months old, a girl, healthy. Do you want her? I was completely overwhelmed.

At that moment I knew there was no going back. A baby was no longer a theoretical thing. She was real, and she was here. That was August of 1990. Lia, the adoption consultant, was well connected and worked hard, but it still wasn't until November that I was able to go down. At that point Grace was five months old. I hadn't met her, hadn't had a picture of her, but ever since first hearing the news, she had been very real to me.

(CPR)

On February 25 I got the call. I was at work that day and alone in the classroom—my kids were off at gym class. There was a telephone at my desk, and the office routed the call through to me. I'll never forget it. A man at my adoption agency was on the line. He said,

"Susan? I have a baby girl for you." He gave me the birthmother's name, told me the baby's birth date and her weight. That was it; that was all the information he had for me.

I sat there after the phone call, just sat ... I had to feel the whole thing first. And then I thought, I have to do something. I have to tell people. So I made a birth announcement: a sign that said "It's a girl!" I went over and hung it in the teachers' lounge. And then of course, I told my kids. I shared a lot with my class; they became really special to me throughout that whole time. As part of my curriculum, I teach a lot about acceptance, of individual differences, of different kinds of families. I explained that adoption is another way of forming a loving family. I had told them that I was going to adopt, and so with this news they knew I'd have to leave them before the end of the school year, but it was OK; the bonus was that they got to go through the anticipation and excitement with me. **(ST)**

Hearing about my daughter happened very fast. I finished and submitted all my paperwork for China around the first of August and then left for vacation with relatives in New Jersey around the fifteenth. I had been there a couple of weeks when I started getting telephone calls from someone who my family said wouldn't leave a message. I didn't think much of it; the weather was beautiful, and I was too busy bicycling or walking or lying on the beach. Finally, I was home one day when the phone rang. It was my social worker at the adoption agency. I thought, oh no! Some of my paperwork needs to be redone. GROAN! She said, "Are you sitting down?" I thought, great. Something's REALLY wrong. "OK, what is it?" I asked. "I'm calling to say that you have a daughter," she said.

I was just stunned. It was so soon—I never expected she was calling with a referral! I tried so hard not to say "You're kidding!" because she'd told me once that "you're kidding!" was the usual response she got to such news. "And," she'd said, "I would never kid about that!" **(MEM)**

We have two children from Colombia. Now we have a situation where we will be adopting a third. She's been born, and we're gathering together the documentation so we can travel.

I think it's every adoptive parent's fantasy that your child's birthparent contacts you again. It rarely happens ... but it happened to us. Not long ago, we received a phone call from the orphanage that placed both our sons with us. My first reaction was, Oh no! Is there some kind of problem? No, they said. But your younger son's birthmother has given birth to a little girl, and we would like to know if you wish to adopt her? I went into shock. Yes, we will take her, I said. No, they said, talk it over with your husband first.

Well, we did talk about it, long and hard. It was very, very difficult. We're in our late thirties, our youngest son is two, and we thought we were leaving babyhood behind. We were closing doors on diapers, cribs, baby things. We had just sold our house. We weren't prepared for another child. We really didn't have the money, didn't have any paperwork—we thought we'd never again have to deal with Immigration and Naturalization! But it was the chance for one of our sons to have a genetic sibling. And it was our only chance to have a girl. It was a heart-wrenching decision, considering our lives at the time, but we did say yes.

Each child changes the family completely, and this one will, in a big way. Colombia has altered its requirements since we adopted our two boys. Now, I'll have to stay in Bogotá for probably four weeks, if all goes well, and I'll probably have the boys with me. My husband will be back up here, moving us. When we return, we'll be returning to a completely new house in a new state. With a new baby. And we're doing all the paperwork backwards—usually with Colombia your immigration work is already done before a child is identified for you. So the process, as well as the transition, is going to be tough.

I don't know any foreign adoptions that go totally smoothly. Like the pain of birth, though, the memory of the difficult times fades after a while. That's happened with our two sons, and it will happen again, once our daughter comes home and life settles down again.

Life is always throwing curveballs. **(MD)**

Jean's Journal

October 10, 1988

Dear Jessie,

When Julie, the social worker, came to see the house last week, she asked me how I felt about myself as I adopt a child. I have this picture, I told her, of standing outside myself, looking at a tall and slender woman holding the hand of a very small child with dark eyes. And I think, "That's right. That woman can do this thing. She *should* do this thing. They will be fine together." And then, I get back into my body and realize that the calm, self-confident woman I was looking at is me, someone who is not sleeping at all well these last few days as the idea of a child gradually becomes more real.

So I ask myself: What is there to be afraid of? I surprise myself to realize that I am already afraid of losing you, of losing the brief sweet time that is ours, even the few days or weeks between when you are born and when I can come for you. Afraid that your birthmother will realize at the last moment how precious you are, how impossible to let go. And afraid of what seems to me the almost inevitable day when you will want to go back to where you were born, to look for the biological family you were a part of, however briefly. I will keep no secrets from you about them or about your status; you will grow up knowing that being adopted is simply a fact of your life, like having brown eyes. But being adopted *is* more than eye color, and we will both know that. Will the day come when you, exasperated with me as a parent, will want to go "home" to that place and people?

No matter how excited and apprehensive I become, I am absolutely certain about this: I want you in my life. However things change, and they surely will in ways I both look forward to and dread, I have no doubt about how much I will always love you, how much I love the idea of you already. It's just that when people are older, little one, we have more experience with change and loss, and so perhaps more fear of them. If we're lucky, we may also know more about love, about its costs and its infinite rewards. I know I will be a different mother to you because I am no longer young. I pray God I will also be a better one.

October 23

Dear Jessie,

The homestudy was sent from the Chicago agency to the international adoption agency in Michigan a few days ago, along with both phases of paperwork. The foreign adoption agency will have everything authenticated and translated, with all the appropriate seals and such, and then they will send the packet to Asunción, in Paraguay. After that, I wait. It could take days or weeks to find your biological mother and you, then thirty to forty-five more days before the paperwork has been processed and I can leave for South America.

In the meantime, I try to revive my Spanish. I have borrowed a tape; last night I learned how to say quite nicely, "My luggage has been lost and has gone to Amsterdam." That should be useful in South America. I've always been grateful when I've traveled in foreign countries to have even a few hesitant words and phrases in the native language; however terrible my accent, it gives me a sense that I'm trying to meet people on their own ground. It also gives me a sense that I can manage, or at least minimally comprehend, what is happening around me. A false security probably, but any illusion will be comforting in the midst of the emotional turmoil this particular trip will bring with it. Fortunately, I have almost no ego about trying to speak a foreign language; I just sally forth with a little paperback dictionary, a big smile, and a willingness to make an absolute fool of myself whenever necessary.

There is such joy here about you, Jess. I'm not sure what I expected—dubiousness at best, I suppose, and downright disapproval at worst. (Not about you, love, but about me: "You, Jean? A mother?") Instead, there is only surprise and delight. Well, it is true that my sister was a little hesitant at first: "Isn't that . . . interesting?" she first replied, the pause signifying in the way that my mother's pauses always did that this was an idea that would take some getting used to. But there are amazingly few such pauses among the people I tell. It was my sister's mother-in-law who has helped me understand this. A sweet lady from a small Illinois town, one would expect her, if anyone, to have trouble with this notion of a single woman becoming the mother of a little brown baby. But when I told her, she said (after a few hesitations and pauses, to be sure) that she understood from her own life how important it sometimes becomes to a woman to have children, in whatever way she can. And she kissed me.

November 30

Dear Jessie,

And so the holidays have begun, with no news about you. The urgency that I've felt all summer and fall has somehow subsided. I, of all people, have had an attack of patience. Perhaps it is the certainty I feel that you are on your way, or the hard-won peace in myself about the rightness of this decision, or just the relief that all the paperwork is finally complete, that makes me able to wait now. I try to think of this as a time for grounding, in preparation for the wonderful but frightening disequilibrium you will soon bring to my life.

This time of year is always bittersweet for me, a time to wrap the memories of my family and my childhood around me like a warm cloak against the winter's chill. And this year, as I revisit these memories again, I realize how large a part my parents have played in my decision to make a family with you.

The holiday season in my childhood home began at Halloween, which was the night my mother produced the first batch of Christmas cookies. My father loved the trick-or-treaters; he always seemed to get to the door first, and he questioned every child about his or her costume, what it was and where it came from, before he passed out the candy. Because he was tall and broad shouldered and wore overcoats with immense shoulder pads, the children of the neighborhood called him Winston Churchill. Every year on Halloween they came to our house to tell the stories of their costumes to Winston. One year, I remember my dad rushing out to the store midevening after more than two hundred trick-or-treaters had exhausted his candy supply.

By Thanksgiving, our house was completely in the holiday mode. My mother had, by then, made many dozens of cookies and something I think of as "Calvinist fruitcake," which substituted strong, black coffee for rum. When I woke on Thanksgiving morning, I can still remember the smell of the turkey already in the oven, the steam building up on the inside of cold windows. Later in the day, Papa presided over the carving of the bird; my Uncle Pete said long prayers of thanks for the abundance of our lives; and after dinner we gathered around the piano for the first Christmas carols of the season. My mother, who had a brief career as a professional pianist before she married, usually played, but everyone in the extended family was musical in some way. Except for my poor father, who sheepishly acknowledged every year that he still only played one thing: the tape recorder.

I had Thanksgiving in my house this year, and I gathered around my dining-room table the family that is being made for you. We set your place with the baby silverware of my childhood; and we toasted each other, and you, and finally my parents. And I realized more profoundly than perhaps I ever have that the least significant thing my mother and dad left me was the money to make this adoption possible. The richest parts of my heritage are their memory, and their values, and what they taught me about family and love. Especially at this time of year, I can't imagine not having someone to pass these on to.

December 24

Dearest Jessie,

I am writing just before I leave to sing in the Christmas Eve services at the cathedral. I wonder how things will be next Christmas with a baby to share this magical night with.

I hung little porcelain booties on my Christmas tree this year, still awaiting your name and the date of your birth. It's a beautiful tree, decorated with candles and with the ornaments I have collected all my life, including some from my parents and from my grandmother, the first Jessie Knoll. But when I was planning my annual tree-trimming party this year, it suddenly dawned on me that we needed a tree near the fireplace in my bedroom where Santa Claus will come—it would never do to make him walk all the way to the first floor. So I bought a second tree this year, a little one for the children of my friends to decorate with paper chains and candy canes. Jessie's tree, we call it.

Papa always bought two trees, one big one and one little one, but for very different reasons. He would bring the trees home and disappear with them into the garage, locking the doors from the inside. After a little while we'd hear the sound of sawing and drilling. We knew then that the big tree was in the stand, and my father had made an assessment of its good and bad points. Then, he would drill holes in the trunk and saw branches from the little tree to insert in just the right places. "Only Dad can make a tree," we used to say. When it was just perfect, he'd add the lights, throw open the garage doors with a flourish, and present a beautifully shaped "natural" tree for decoration. An odd confluence of memories: the smell of evergreen, the taste of gingerbread, and the sound of saw and drill.

The presentation of Christmas gifts was almost as important as the gifts themselves. Ribbons and bows were merely the beginning. I remember presents within presents, presents whose functions were undiscoverable without elaborate explanations, and presents in opposite pairs (my mother once gave me an elegant silk bathrobe and bright red clown-style pajamas in the same box). But Papa held the record here, hands down. One year, he gave my mother an electric can opener, and then presented all of her other gifts to her sealed in tin cans.

Christmas is a season of charity, I was taught, preferably anonymous charity. My mother used to put together plates of Christmas treats for "the shut-ins," and I remember my sister and I driving around with her, ringing doorbells and then running away as fast as we could, leaving plates of cookies and fruitcake behind. There was something about the Salvation Army standing in the cold that especially touched my dad, and he had a rule that no one could go shopping downtown without a roll of quarters for the buckets. One year, I thought I'd try to save a few for myself, but Papa caught on and made me empty my stash at the last bucket we saw. Once, I remember I told him how wonderful and unselfish this all was. And he stopped, looked at me very seriously, and said, "This is the most selfish thing I do all year. It makes me feel so good." I remember that whenever people tell me what a wonderful thing I am doing to bring a child from the Third World to be my own. They do not know, as I do, how selfish this really is.

Wherever you are, dearest child, Merry Christmas.

January 31, 1989

"Hello, hello . . . Dr. Knoll? We've had a referral, and Ricardo wants to talk with you."

Click . . . buzz . . .

"Hello, this is Ricardo. We've had a referral a few minutes ago. A three-month-old girl. She is well, seems quite healthy. Her mother has had a difficult postdelivery period . . . anemia . . . hemorrhaging . . . pneumonia. She is not able to keep the child. Would you be interested?"

At first, I ask reasonable questions. "Is the baby all right?" ("Yes, she seems fine.") "What do we know about her?" ("Born full term in a hospital in Asunción. Normal birth weight.")

Then, I begin to cry. "When can I go to her?" I can't remember the answer. I can't remember anything much. Ricardo will leave tomorrow and arrive in Asunción on Thursday morning. He will see the baby Friday. There will be details, and photographs, early next week. The rest is a blur, except . . .

"The lawyer says you would not believe how beautiful this baby is."

"You bet she is," I say with authority about this child I have never seen.

I hang up. What shall I do now? Whom should I tell? I step out of my office, my cheeks still wet with tears. To the first person I see, who looks at my face with horror, I sob, "I'm a mommy!" And people come out of their offices, to hug me and laugh. I wander vaguely in the direction of our reception area. The dean is there. He looks annoyed at first that I should be carrying on so unprofessionally at work. For the moment, I do not much care. I blurt out at him, "I'm a mommy!" The dean hugs me then, repeating over and over, "Don't cry, Jean. This is wonderful!"

Gradually, others gather. It was originally a sad day. A beloved old teacher has died, and many have been to the services. I had intended to go too. But at the last minute there was a student to see. So I was here for the phone call. Arthur would have liked that, that on the day we remembered him, you came to carry on. (He sometimes called himself a "philosophical anarchist." What does that mean for you?) There are hugs and kisses and more tears. You are here, Jessie, after all the months and years of thinking, deciding, waiting . . . delivered to my office.

I spend the next hour on the phone. First, of course, Peggy. Then, Naomi and Lonnie, so that they can finally get a sound night's sleep knowing they are, at last, grandparents. My sister is in school, so I cannot call her till tonight. My friend Catherine cannot be reached at all; she is doing a workshop somewhere in Michigan. But celebrations begin in a dozen other places. I have a double ice-cream cone and a bottle of champagne for dinner.

At long last, I come home. Last weekend the painters were here. They swept through the house with plaster and paint, transforming the second floor. I thought, "Now this is real . . . my life is changed, my house is changed, because of a baby." Your room is painted pink. "Oh, God, Jean, pink is so sexist!" some people say. Maybe, but you will have a lifetime of things mauve and taupe, and I want you to have a few pink years; I did. Last night, I brought home a wicker rocker and set it in the middle of your room, alone on the rug except for a giant stuffed dog, a gift to you from my godchildren. Suddenly, I was seized by the irresistible desire to see your room with a crib in it. There is no crib yet, but there is a Portacrib from my sister, until last night still in its Christmas box. Very late last night I put it together, and made it up with teddy bear sheets. Then I sat in the rocker and rocked for a long time, staring at the empty Portacrib and imagining a head of tousled brown hair moving gently to some dream.

Today, twelve hours later, I have a daughter.

Telephone Calls and Other Connections

commentary

After spending time waiting, sometimes in frustration, the first news of a child seems unbelievably exciting, but almost unreal. I found myself doubting reality one night after getting a midnight telephone call from South America about a baby who had become available for adoption. Was this really happening? Or were we still asleep? By the end of the call we were both wide awake. For the next hour or so, we spread our old atlas out on the bed and hauled out all the documents and papers we'd put together over the last few months, talking until common sense finally told us to go back to bed. The next morning, I remember gazing into my orange juice, marveling at how changed and significant everything felt.

That call was the culmination of several months of meetings, telephone calls, priority mail packages, and a general shift in outlook from hopelessness to determination. Part of this new outlook was putting together a clearer idea of who and what we were looking for. During our homestudy, our agency suggested that we sit down as a family and figure out our "requirements" for this adoption. Meanwhile, we could look at the intercountry adoption programs that they recommended and see if we found any that "fit" our family.

So, over the course of a few days we discussed the situation. We all agreed that we wanted to adopt a baby, no older than six months; that ruled out a couple of programs that only placed children two years and older. We drew the line on one program that placed only boys because our son specifically asked if we could look for a baby sister. There was a program in Thailand that placed infants, but the children came from orphanages and there was no contact possible with the children's birthparents. That, Peter and I decided, was something we saw as a requirement for this adoption (for reasons to be explained later in this chapter). A program that placed Honduran infants wasn't right, either, because it was an "escort" program—meaning we would not travel to Honduras, but the baby would be flown to the United States under the care of an escort. We had decided that we wanted an adoption program that would require travel to our new child's place of birth. Finally, another program didn't sound right because it would take at least a year for our application even to be processed; and all three of us were unanimous that we wanted a new child in our lives as soon as possible.

And then there was a Peruvian adoption program, based in another state. This program, we read, would accept us as applicants if we had a completed, approved homestudy. We had to be willing to stay in Peru until the adoption was complete. Families with children already were OK (as were singles). Waiting children were of both sexes and ranged in age from newborn to eight or even older. And though the agency helped adopters with many of the preadoption details, basically each adoption was an independent one, meaning that there would probably be some contact with the child's birthfamily. And there were many children in Peru waiting for new families—the wait could be a short one.

It wasn't long before Peter and I were on the telephone. One of the program's staff explained to us during the initial call that they employed "adoption coordinators" who worked in several South and Central American countries, people who were native to those countries and whose job it was to make contact with birthparents wishing to relinquish children for adoption. In turn, the coordinators worked with the U.S. office in matching waiting children and prospective families. The office staff in the United States helped adopters assemble all the documents required for an intercountry adoption, and the coordinator's job was to oversee each adoption "on-site" in each country: the coordinator would link up adopters with translators and lawyers, find adoptive families a place to stay while in the country, and advise adopters of U.S. visa requirements once their child's adoption process was complete.

With the hope that this program was as good as it sounded, we sent in our application, the required fee, and soon after, our completed homestudy. Very quickly, our involvement shifted from our first "homestudy agency" to this new program and—most importantly—to the adoption coordinator assigned to us. Although the U.S. office of the program was important to us, it quickly became clear that the key to this whole arrangement would be our coordinator. And as we talked with her during her trips to the States and when she was back in Peru, she became an essential presence in our lives. We wondered when she would call next. We wrote down questions to ask her. We tried not to sound too anxious or pushy or take too much of her time during overseas phone calls. And she in turn would answer our questions and give us information that would keep us excited or fearful or mystified or reassured for days. From the perspective I have now, I see that she was truly functioning as a "midwife": she was preparing us and assisting us in creating this new family; she was the guide who would ultimately be there to bring us and our new child together. She was our link between our past and our future.

And she had been the voice over the telephone last night. As I thought back over the news we had gotten, it seemed I could remember every detail of the conversation—the hesitations, the jumbled questions and answers, and the echo of our voices over the long-distance line.

Adoptive parents usually do remember "the phone call" with great clarity. Afterward, every detail having to do with receiving such profound news becomes precious. For me, it's the scrap of paper on which we scribbled our daughter Cristina's name as we heard it over the telephone for the very first time. I must admit that I also saved my lists of things to do and telephone bills showing all the calls we made to spread the news. Our adoption coordinator was our human link between past and present, but these scraps of paper are links of a different sort: ones that we can touch and read and that bear witness to the joining of Cristina's—and our—Life Before and Life After. They are the recorded beginnings of an event important and very precious to us all. It's second nature to me to save these things; my grandmother also saved scraps of Life Before. Images and records of her birthplace across the ocean in Ireland and her particular family history are recorded in an old album of hers that I have. Embedded in old receipts, photos, and pressed flowers are memories—ephemeral perhaps, but nonetheless alive and familiar to her and now me through her scrapbook and the casual family connections I take for granted. At first I thought I was saving all this stuff only for myself, but now I know I also do it for my children, to give them a sense of how they got to be here.

I was musing about all this last Monday morning. We had just returned from a weekend with my aunt and uncle, and in my head I was recalling their familiar faces—road maps of Life Before. Grandpa's nose, I realized, comes through in Uncle Joe, and in my cousins Steve, Erica, and Chris. Susan has her mother's smile. My eyes came from my father, and my son looks like pictures of me at the same age. My daughter . . .

Comes from Peru, and looks like her birthmother.

Well, of course, I know that, I thought with confusion. What startled me was a split second of experiencing what it will feel like for Cristina when she tries to reach back to her Life Before, to the generations that preceded her. The sensation of an empty, un-answering space frightened me. How, I thought, will she be able to handle this? And how will I be able to help her cope with that loss—I, who have never questioned the easy access to my genetic past?

I thought of something another adoptive parent told me recently. While she was in South America, she had met another parent also waiting for her baby's adoption to be completed. When my friend asked this woman if she had visited the nearby historic sites or seen any of the city in which she had spent the last month, the woman shrugged. "Why should I?" she said. "I don't understand the language, and it's hard to get around. Besides, when we get home, all this won't matter much to my baby. He'll be an American."

As incredulous as I am at this remark, I want to believe that this parent didn't really understand the implications of her attitude, or was simply overwhelmed by her immediate situation. After all, life as a new parent struggling with temporary life in a foreign country, unfamiliar language and food, and the added burden of appoint-ments and court appearances, can be tough. But how I worry about her little boy! His Life Before involves a history that will be hard enough to understand as a young child without having even a few scraps of information or photos. When he's eight years old and is beginning to ask about his origins, will his parents have anything to tell him or give him, not even a good memory of the place he was born or the people who share his culture? Will they have to say that they considered all that unimportant?

Some of us know only the whys and none of the whos about our children's past. ("Your birthmother had a difficult postdelivery," Jean might find herself saying one day. "I was told about her anemia . . . hemorrhaging . . . pneumonia . . . and that she wasn't able to care for a child.") But all of us who've adopted abroad and traveled to meet our child there have been able to live in the country of our child's birth, if even for only a few days. What we absorb of our child's culture and the memories we bring back may be the sum total of what we can pass on to him, all that we will have to help him fill that big empty space that should hold some record of his genetic heritage. It's very likely that our adult recollections of time spent in his country of birth will become his connection to Life Before, and will be as priceless for him as the memory of the phone call announcing his arrival is for us.

Spending time waiting for news of your child is an important luxury. It's time given to you for planning just how you want to collect and preserve the special information you will assemble about her heritage. Even if you know in advance that your child will be assigned to you from an orphanage, there will still be information you can gather about her background that will be important for her. One essential fact to remember in such a case is that children aren't usually simply "abandoned." In many countries where there is no established system for child placement, abandonment is simply the method many mothers use to make an adoption plan for their children. The social stigma of bearing a child out of wedlock can also mean that the child must be relinquished anonymously. In any case, most "abandoned" children aren't left without any thought for their safety or care, as the term implies. In fact, leaving a child at a business, on the steps of a police station, or at the door of an orphanage may be the most responsible thing a parent without any resources can do. This is vital for your child to know.

A child without identified birthparents will at least have either orphanage workers or foster caregivers who have looked after her.

Your lawyer, the adoption coordinator, and even the social worker who will interview you in the process of the adoption there will also have had contact with your child. Finally, even if you don't meet your child's birthparents, you may have the privilege of meeting other members of her family.

Each of these people, no matter how small their involvement with your child, is part of her history, and their names and images will provide her in future years with some sense of a cultural background at least, and a genetic background at best. Even if you don't intend to keep in contact with any of them, at the very least make sure to learn and write down their names and plan to take their picture, so she will have, combined with the stories you can tell her, a clearer concept about her Life Before and her adoption. Depending on the circumstances you may want to establish a correspondence with the caregivers and contacts you meet after you're back home, or send supplies or gifts to them and other children in their care. Many people decide to record their experiences in a journal, as Jean did. You may want to bring along a small tape recorder so that people close to your child, especially her foster caregivers, can record their memories of her or tape a special message for her to hear when she is older. And again, don't forget to take pictures—lots of them. Photograph not just you and your little one but the people around you, the place you stay, the street vendor at the corner, and the church up the street. It takes some courage; my husband recalls how conspicuous he felt while walking through the streets snapping pictures, armed with a bright blue knapsack and pushing Cristina in a stroller. Yet for all the pictures we took, we both regret not taking more. Now, thousands of miles away and unsure of when we will return to South America, I wish we had risked more stares and gotten twice as many photos of all the places and people around us—as many images as possible to give our daughter a sense of her past history.

~

Another reason why we went international is that we were uncomfortable about the birthparent issue. We had concerns with domestic adoption in that respect, not knowing what a relationship with a birthparent might be. With intercountry adoption, we knew that issue would probably not be there for us. **(DE)**

When I thought about the birthmother of my child, I didn't even want to know this person, didn't want to face the fact that my potential son came from another human being. Then I was told that by Peruvian law we would have to meet her. I was terribly unsure about all this. But we had some reassurance; we had friends who had come back from Peru with a very positive story about their child's birthmother. Having been forced into the relationship, though, I did find out that I liked and admired her . . . and our involvement with her completely changed our sense of the adoption, and of our whole lives. **(FJ)**

I wasn't able to get much of a sense of our children's early life. There wasn't any opportunity to spend time with the orphanage workers, and you're discouraged from asking too many questions. You can have a picture of your child's birthmother, but you have to ask. That's pretty much it. Adoption in Colombia is like it was here in the 1960s. There is still a lot of secrecy, protection of information, sealed records, and so on. There was a mothers' building where birthmoms stay. But the conversation was cut off quickly when I asked a question or two about it. They see it as none of the adoptive parents' business. **(MD)**

I had a good relationship with Gracie's orphanage and was especially assured by the obvious affection the staff had for her. But I wanted more. I tried like crazy to get information about Gracie's birthparents, but constantly ran up against a brick wall. "They don't keep records here and don't worry, the birthmother won't give you any trouble," the coordinator told me; she completely misunderstood my questions. The concept of wanting to know for my child and for myself seemed totally foreign to her and to others I spoke with in Honduras. I persisted, though, and got an appointment with the hospital's records manager. She told me that all the records they had of my child's birth were transferred to the orphanage, and if the orphanage had nothing more than the name the birthmother gave and her address (which was probably false), then that's all the information that exists. Look, someone finally told me, Grace's birthmother was probably a young girl from the mountains who came to the city, gave birth, and left. But she was smart enough and loving enough to do it in a hospital, from where she knew her child would go into at least government care and maybe even into a good adoptive home.

So that's what I know about Grace's birthparents. That's what I can tell her. I so wish it were more.   **(PR)**

When you adopt from India, there is no contact with birthparents. Often, children born at birthing centers to young unmarried mothers are abandoned at birth. Identities are masked on relinquishment papers or any other documents. Is there a chance of finding them again? It's unlikely. Fourteen million people live in Calcutta—these girls leave and are swallowed up by the city.   **(NA)**

Each child has a record at their Korean agency. Their births are also entered into the government birth registry but the certificate may or may not have birthparent names, and those names might be false, anyway. A woman will typically hide information about an out-of-wedlock birth at all costs and would never dare to keep the child. The society is very Confucian and paternalistic. The bloodline is all, and each person has a document showing his genealogical background that he needs for entering school, applying for a job, and so on. Children born without a bloodline are severely disadvantaged, and these are the children who come to us in international adoption.

Once in a while, birthparents will return to agencies to check up on their children. They have full access to the file, but they're not given any identifying information about adoptive families. In our case, we've made sure that our names and addresses are all over everything we send to the agency for our children's files, so that if their birthmother wants to, she can get in touch with us. That's one way to try to make contact.   **(PM)**

Every adoption is a tragedy, I believe. I cannot say that tragedy is positive. But some aspects of tragedy are incredible. And I know that the most incredible aspect of Hannah's adoption is that she is blessed with a birthmother who is amazing and courageous and strong. She truly believed, and told me so several times, that she wanted her daughter to have a better life than she had or would have. That's why she made the decision for Hannah's adoption.

In the first few days I knew Hannah's birthmother, I found out through the interpreter that she hadn't eaten for days. I was appalled. But I wondered, too, Was she lying to me? Was she "on the take," like people had warned me? No. When I gave her some money, she looked at me directly, and said, "I know that my daughter will never have to beg for food like I have done." I never doubted her, or her conviction.

One day early on in the adoption process, Hannah's birthmother came to my hotel. I invited her in, but she only indicated that she wanted to see the baby. I was nervous, not knowing what she wanted. But I went and got Hannah, who was sleeping, and brought her down. She looked closely at the baby and felt her legs carefully. Then she looked at me and smiled and left. I was really puzzled, until later my interpreter explained that she had come to make sure I was taking care of Hannah properly and feeding her enough. I never denied her contact with the baby afterward; I knew I had nothing to fear.   **(ST)**

I first met my child's birthmother at my adoption coordinator's office the evening I arrived in the country. We met, and she handed my baby to me. Then we each signed a document stating that she was relinquishing her baby to me of her own free will. The baby's footprint was taken.

It was hard, the relinquishment. I could only imagine what this mother was going through. I'm sure it was very painful for her, but she didn't show much emotion. And yet this was a mother who had breastfed her baby for four days. But there were few tears. Maybe it was shock, or maybe it was culture: I think people don't cry very openly down there.

I had a difficult relationship with her. She was very demanding and I didn't know where to draw the line on her demands. My lawyer helped me a little, but basically I was on my own to try to figure out how to cope with her. I was frightened that she would take my son back. And the thought of losing Nathan was terrifying.

At one point she requested through the lawyer that I let Nathan come and visit her for the day, alone. I couldn't agree to that. Our compromise was that he would come, but that I would accompany him (I also arranged to have an escort bring me and stay with us). So one day we spent the day in her shack, in one of the Lima slums. It was really tough—the conditions were marginal. She had four other kids and lived in one room with a rough concrete floor. It was good to spend the whole day together, and I did get a sense of who she was and what her life was like. But I will say that I went through hell that day.   **(FS)**

It was often very awkward. There was always this unspoken tension between us—I was afraid she might change her mind and that thought kept me from getting too close to her. But throughout the time I was there she visited often, and never gave any indication she would change her mind. She simply wanted to see the baby. I understand that now, but my fear kept me from seeing it then.

She was very young, and just like any American girl, she saw that a baby just couldn't fit into her life. It wasn't that she had any big career plans; in fact, she wasn't interested in working, as far as I could tell. I think she spent most of her days hanging out with her friends. My lawyer was keeping an eye on her and paid for a place for her to spend her nights. So in some way, this adoption gave her a little stability. Otherwise she might have been out on the street.

Despite my fear of her, I enjoyed her. I really did. And I think—I know—she liked me. Otherwise my daughter might not have come home with me. She was smart, and she was tough. But she was soft, too; she was a mother. And so was I. We shared our child for the time that I was there, and especially because we got to know and respect each other, we still share her. And that's OK. Because I want my daughter to be proud of her beautiful, strong, and very loving roots.   **(LVP)**

~

No one can predict the future of intercountry adoption procedures, but traveling to a child's birthplace to complete his adoption may well become the norm in intercountry adoption. Though some countries still allow children to be escorted by a caretaker to the United States, most require that adoptive parents show their commitment to the child and to the adoption by initiating adoption proceedings in the child's birth country. In this way the government can verify through social workers and through the judicial process that the parents are who their documents say they are; any questions about their credentials can be asked and answered in person. If there are difficulties in adjustment between parents and child or if the parents have serious misgivings about the adoption after meeting the child, those doubts can be addressed before the child leaves his home country. It also goes without saying that a poor country benefits economically from the money adoptive families spend during their stay, perhaps another reason for requiring adopters to travel, sometimes twice, to their child's birth country.

The length of a visit varies according to the rules of each country, but whether it is two weeks or six months, and no matter how long the stay or how frustrating it may seem, each moment is an important opportunity to develop a relationship, personal and sometimes familial, with a child's past.

I emphasize familial because there may be an opportunity to meet your child's birthparents (typically, only her birthmother). If this possibility makes you uneasy, you're not alone. Many people feel that keeping a child's birth connections anonymous or at a distance is a far more comfortable way to treat the very real fact that, as an adoptee, a child actually has more than one or two parents. This is a threatening statement for many adoptive parents and, unfortunately, a motivating force for some to choose inter-country adoption, where connections between birthparents and children in some cases are permanently severed due to abandonment or death. But is "the less confused she is about who her parents are, the better" a good way to approach this issue? I'm not sure.

This attitude may work well when your child is very young. But in intercountry adoption, children and parents simply don't resemble one another. As a child grows older and more aware of her differences and origins, she will have a growing number of questions for her parents. And in the absence of any information, a child may form impressions of her origins that are erroneous and ultimately unfair—to herself, her parents, and her birthparents. If you are lucky enough to get correct information about your child's past directly from her birthmother, it will be of immeasurable value as the years progress and your child's emotional needs grow and change.

A meeting with your child's birthparent, if at all possible, is also beneficial to the birthmother. As you prepare to travel to meet your child, you will undoubtedly experience, amidst the excitement and anticipation, a good amount of fear about the unknown future and doubt over your decision. If you can imagine these feelings deeply intensified, you will have some idea of what your child's birthmother has certainly felt. For her, meeting you could be extraordinarily painful—but ultimately reassuring. If you believe yourself to be a good person who will be a loving parent and can personally assure her of a safe and happy future for her child, you will give her a huge amount of comfort. No one should have to make the decision she has had to make. And no one should be denied the opportunity to see that such a painful decision could also be a positive one.

Relationships with birthparents vary widely, if the quotes above are any indication, and can be difficult, especially at first. Dealing with the very person who has made you a parent but who also has the power to take away that privilege creates a tension unlike any you may ever have experienced. Such strain often limits contact and intimacy and in worst cases causes resentment that carries over into a negative opinion of the birthparent that a child hears later from her adoptive parents.

Distrust may develop between parties if birthparents press for more contact or payments of cash above and beyond what the adoptive parents expect to give. Even though the situation may put you on guard, it's important to keep the requests in perspective. Sometimes birthparents make demands because intermediaries (adoption coordinators or lawyers) have made promises to them that haven't been kept. And if a birthmother has been promised help with some basic human needs and that help hasn't materialized, the adoptive parent is the natural person to appeal to. This isn't to say that birthparents (or adoptive parents) have the right to push the other to the edge on any issue. Intimidation has no place in adoption, and mediation by a trustworthy adoption worker, social worker, or lawyer should be sought at once. This isn't always an easy situation in a foreign environment, and it can become immediately apparent that limits on contact are necessary as soon as possible until the conflict is resolved. In any case, it's good practice to agree on a plan for visits and exchange of information between adoptive parents, child, and birthparents from the beginning so that everyone has the same expectations and no one's privacy is violated. Despite your best-laid plans, though, it could also be that the birthmother will find any more than the very minimum of contact too painful.

In many cases birthparents and adoptive parents form a bond that is forged by their mutual love for the child, and becomes stronger if all parents maintain a respect for each other and for their different cultures. Such a positive relationship can, despite the difficult circumstances of some intercountry adoptions, become the central experience of the adoption for adoptive families.

This said, it must be noted that changing adoption policies of different countries may in fact make it much harder to have contact with a child's birthparents. Because relationships between birth- and adoptive parents, due to the emotional content of the relationship, can become a means of financial gain, and because there is far more room for illegal maneuvering in a situation where a child, precious beyond words, is the central issue, countries are moving toward policies that keep birth- and adoptive parents one step removed from each other through state regulation. However, if there is even a small possibility of having some contact with your child's birthmother and if you believe that the feelings of everyone involved in this very personal transaction should be considered, then you should prepare to ask, as politely and persistently as possible, for an opportunity to meet and talk with your child's birthmother. Any future contact you might want to have with her will involve barriers of time, distance, and language; those are reason enough to seek her out while you are in her country.

You may not be comfortable with all this. I certainly wasn't. Like many adoptive parents, I pictured The Birthmother as a hazy person in the background, several steps behind the clear dream-image of the family we would create by adopting a child. Because I suspected that tremendous emotions would be involved in meeting her, it felt safer to keep her out of focus. I'd read about adoption, about how it would be for our family once we brought our new child home and what growing up adopted was all about. But I hadn't read much about the feelings a birthmother has, so I was completely unprepared for the intensity of meeting her and unsure of what to do and what to say. My fear that she might change her mind about Cristina's adoption left me even more unsure. In retrospect, I wish I had paid less attention to my fears, as difficult as I know that might have been. Now, I look back on all our adoption preparations and regret that we hadn't realized how important it would be to us and to Cristina to have known her birthmother better.

I heard a birthmother speak recently. "Every mother," she said, "is entitled to know that her child is safe, healthy, and loved." For many birthparents in foreign countries, the only assurance they will ever have of these three important things is the assumption that the institution or system they relinquished their child to will provide for them. If instead birthparents actually have the opportunity to meet the adoptive parents who indeed provide safety, health, and love for their children, they will be spared much anguish.

Even if you are not sure you will meet your child's birthmother, assume you might, and make some simple and thoughtful preparations. It will help to spend some time in advance learning how to express your gratitude simply in the language of your child's birthmother (find someone to help you with this, and write it down, to be safe). Have a special gift of remembrance ready to present to her, something very personal that she will always keep. Bring along pictures of your home and family. At your first meeting, you may feel that anything you say or do will just be too superficial, but in fact a certain amount of planned ceremony may help you get through the hard moments. Taking a few photographs can and should be part of the meeting, even if you feel it will be out of place in the midst of so much emotion. In fact, it will be easier if you hand your camera to someone else to take a photo of birth- and adoptive parents and child—an extremely important document for everyone to have (afterward, a copy should be given to the birthparent). Finally, if everyone is agreeable, arrange for another meeting and try to save most questions for that time.

The decision your child's birthmother makes takes a great deal of courage. In the United States, birthparents are beginning to get the recognition they deserve for taking such a difficult step; it's not yet so in other areas of the world. In Asia, this attitude is so strong and culturally embedded that abandonment is the only option for young girls who have "shamed" themselves in this way. In Latin America, such cultural attitudes are not that strong, but there is still clear disapproval of the option of adoption. Criticism of mothers who decide on adoption for their children is wrapped up in the traditional assumption that it is primarily the woman's responsibility to somehow provide for her children no matter how desperate her circumstances. Such attitudes are responsible for the lack of respect many birthmothers experience during this whole process. One of the best gifts you can give her is your attempt to understand the difficult decision she has made. No one who has borne a child can ever let go easily, and once you become a parent, you, too, will know just how painful it must be.

In the familiar surroundings of my own country, I can remember the confusing emotions provoked by the first news about our daughter. Of course it was exciting, but I didn't instantly feel that "it was meant to be," as I had heard some adoptive parents talk about their children. I worried throughout the days of preparation for travel. I wondered about our "right" to this child. Knowing of the powerlessness of so many poor Latin Americans (Cristina's birthmother among them), and after reading about the losses involved in adoption, I feared—at that late date—that both adoption and Latin America would just be too overwhelming for me and my family. At one point, we had dinner with friends who had adopted a Peruvian baby. I remember a mostly happy discussion, centering on their two-month stay and their beautiful new daughter, but the notes I took during our conversation with them are riddled with doubt and fear: question marks, warnings, and underlining. "Don't" and "never" jump up at me as I reread my scribbles. It's obvious that at the same time I was preparing to open my arms to my new daughter and the culture she would bring with her, I was also expecting to assume some sort of siege mentality to get through the process. I wish that, all practical warnings for everyday life in a foreign country aside, I had spent more time worrying about and planning ways we could connect with Cristina's Life Before.

Looking back, I now realize that those who knew nothing about all the what-ifs that plagued me, who simply believed in our ability to become parents in this way, ultimately gave me hope. Their comfort and assurance—and even their ignorance of the often shaky character of Third-World politics—restored my optimism as we approached our date of departure. We needed their faith, for there were times when it seemed that larger political forces beyond our control would determine if we would successfully emerge from this experience a family.

"Up and Down All at Once"

voices

A fter completing our paperwork for a Peruvian adoption but having had no luck with a placement, our local agency called us in mid-December with a domestic adoption placement. The birthmother was due in about a week. But we had funny feelings about the situation. The mother admitted to abusing alcohol several times during the pregnancy. That was a red flag, since both of us had alcoholic parents. We wanted that legacy to stop. Yet . . . this placement was ours for the taking if we said yes.

We needed guidance. Neither of us are churchgoers, but two Sundays in a row we went to church. We were looking for community, for support in this very difficult decision. The first Sunday, we went to a Unitarian church. The sermon was all about the upcoming solstice: the shortest day and longest night of the year. About having an age-old faith that a seed of life is truly planted in darkness. The next Sunday we went to a Congregational church. The theme of that sermon was that when God calls upon you to do something, you do it.

We were thrown into a great quandary. Was this potential adoption the seed of light in the midst of our darkness? And was God calling upon us to do something here? Should we say yes to the universe? If we say no, will such a situation happen for us ever again?

In the end, we could not accept the placement. It wasn't right, even if God was telling us to do it. Once again, we were back with Peru. For which we had no placement at all.

After we had made our decision, I read a quote of Carl Jung's that went something like: the more we live in the realm of our subconscious and imagination, the richer we will be. With that idea I suddenly saw the connection between the solstice seed of light and the unknown world of Peru, amidst our darkness of indecision and worry. We were going to do it; we were going to take the leap for Peru.

And we did. One week after we refused the domestic adoption, our son was born in Lima, Peru.   **(FJ)**

The most stressful part of the adoption was that my contacts were overly optimistic—don't worry, you will have a referral in three months ... well, maybe by September ... by Thanksgiving perhaps ... It's February, and your baby has been born! She'll be home by March ... April ... May ...

But I was a believer. I had friends who had adopted, and they told me look, it will happen. Sometimes it just takes a while for the right baby to find the right parent. I really carried that hope with me, despite the delays, the wait. Other friends who weren't familiar with international adoption didn't really understand the reasons for all the delays but could see that it was hard and were very protective of me. They didn't want to see me hurt and they worried. Nobody ever came right out and said it, but I suspect some of them never believed I would ever end up with a child. But my response to their worry was to tell them that I knew it would happen, that I believed in international adoption. Answering their concerns helped me validate my decision to adopt in this way.

People assume that since international adoption can involve so much red tape, false starts, or temporary standstills, you've somehow been taken for a ride, you're going through illegal channels, and so on. That does and doesn't happen, and I think the adoption process I experienced is a good example. First, I talked with a recommended out-of-state agency. They seemed OK on the telephone. But the paperwork I got from them—especially the contracts they wanted me to sign—didn't seem right. Maybe it sounds trivial, but all the forms were badly photocopied and loaded with typos. It seemed like a pretty informal operation for something as big and serious as adoption. But what made me really uncomfortable was that they wanted me to pay a big chunk of money up front with nothing more than some vague information about their programs in different countries and that they had had very satisfying results. It just didn't seem trustworthy. So I didn't go with them; and it's a good thing, since not too long after I heard they'd been shut down by their state's attorney general for all kinds of misrepresentation and broken promises.

I didn't go with that agency ultimately because of some advice I received, and everyone who adopts should hear the same thing: "If a situation doesn't feel right to you, go with your gut." In other words, pay attention if you're feeling uneasy. You do have to trust your instincts.

Next, I tried to adopt through an individual contact I made in Mexico. At first it all sounded very promising. The woman I was dealing with said that she knew of two pregnant birthmothers who wanted to place their children for adoption, but not too long after that she said the babies were unavailable for different reasons, and then ... I didn't hear anything again. That was very hard, since I had been told to leave on a moment's notice and had gone out and bought baby clothes and other stuff. I lost several months with that situation and began to feel discouraged.

Finally I made contact with a good adoption coordinator, someone who worked independent of any agencies. She was based in Guatemala. I was unable to travel there, which meant that I had to put a lot of trust in her and her connections. It did ultimately work—a baby was identified for me! Then once again I found myself waiting for the paperwork to be completed ... then I waited some more ... I waited for six months in all. At the end of the wait, it turned out that the baby's arrival in the United States was delayed because they were waiting for another child to get processed so the two could share the same escort on the trip to the States; it would be cheaper that way.

The final ironic frustration was that the escort and the two children missed their connection in Miami. So my family and I waited—once again—in Newark airport for a baby who they thought, I'm sure, didn't even exist.

The process was at times very difficult. But I know others have gone through worse, and in retrospect I feel lucky nothing more than a couple of stops and starts and a long wait were the only things that happened to me.   **(RJ)**

With our second child, Colombia's new rules stated that U.S. agencies and the homestudies done by them now had to be approved by Bienestar Familiar (the Colombian government agency that oversees all adoptions). And only those agencies on a special Bienestar list could arrange intercountry adoptions. But no agencies in our state of New Hampshire were on that list. We went back and forth on this with the orphanage in Bogotá and with Bienestar, then finally settled on an agreeable out-of-state agency. Then a crazy thing happened just before our homestudy was completed: that agency, for some mysterious reason, was taken off the Bienestar list! The orphanage wrote to suggest another agency . . . in Washington state. Is this place near you? they asked.

After more weeks of negotiating, the orphanage and Bienestar compromised on a local New Hampshire agency to oversee the adoption. But just as we were completing the processing, our agency's license expired and had to be renewed. Bienestar called another halt to our process. Relicensing usually takes months in our state, and Bienestar would not approve our application and homestudy unless our agency was in good standing. I called the licensing bureau and pleaded. Through my efforts, the license was granted months early. I went personally to the state capital to get a signed certification. Finally, our homestudy could be sent down to Bogotá. At that point, I would have done anything. We had waited long enough.   **(MD)**

We had a scary incident as we were returning home from starting up our second child's adoption in Paraguay. As we waited to board the plane, the police suddenly took us aside and demanded to see the Paraguayan passport of our older daughter Marisa (who was with us and whom we had adopted three years earlier). We of course had her U.S. passport and hadn't thought we'd need the old Paraguayan passport, so we hadn't brought it. We did have all her original adoption documentation with us in case of an emergency, but it was packed away with our luggage. I vividly remember Marisa pushed into a corner while we frantically tried to communicate with the police. I panicked, thinking, here we are leaving our new daughter behind for who knows how long, and now what's happening with Marisa? We were so scared. Luckily, someone came along who spoke Spanish and English and worked with us and the police until the situation was ironed out. But we were scared. When we returned a few months later, we made sure to pack that Paraguayan passport!   **(DE)**

Our second adoption from Korea was more problematic. We were offered a child who had a lot of medical complications. At the time we had to make the decision about her, my husband, who is a house builder, had just fallen off the roof of a barn and was in the hospital. I was left with the information and basically had to make the decision for this child on my own. There were major concerns—first, how would we deal with her illness? Second, would our insurance cover her condition? I just went round and round, talking with medical people and insurance people. I took her medical information to a doctor in the city. He told me she was very much an at-risk child; he wasn't at all encouraging. It was an extremely difficult decision, and the stress was really hard to take—I was running around, shuttling between my husband in the hospital and a series of doctors in order to get an opinion on this child. The insurance company told me that they couldn't cover her (preexisting) condition. I thought about switching insurance companies. But that wasn't going to work because of all the hospitalization my husband was going through.

I finally had to decide against this child. It was so very difficult—she was partly home, as far as I was concerned. I went through such guilt over the situation for a long time. And then I somehow didn't feel entitled to ask for a second chance. And there was the fear that we would never be able to adopt another child if we had turned down a placement. **(FEM)**

I had envisioned this adoption to be a spiritual journey. But in reality it was a very stressful experience. The idea of it was spiritual, not the trip itself. The day I got to Moscow, a Russian editorial appeared in the newspaper questioning the practice of "selling" Russian children to foreigners. In response, the *oblast*, or county commissioner, put a moratorium on children under his directorate. I had a plane ticket that stipulated I was to leave exactly two weeks after I arrived, so I had a deadline. And there was this brick wall to deal with. I was very fortunate in that I had very good adoption facilitators who pushed for me, day by day, but it never seemed like a promising situation. When you approach a desk and find a court official counting with an abacus, you have some idea of the primitive conditions under which so many officials work there. That, for me, was a metaphor for how things are handled in Russia.

Because of all the difficulties, I felt I was robbed of anticipation. There was just the most incredible feeling of desperation. Always waiting to hear from my facilitators what the situation was. I tried out some cultural diversions; I went to the ballet twice. But as I sat there I knew that my son was alone in his orphanage and he was aware that I existed, and I wanted to be with him. My goodness, I'm in Russia! I kept thinking. The culture is so rich and there's so much to do ... but I couldn't concentrate.

You know, in our culture if something is going wrong, you complain to the manager. There isn't any of that in Russia. That "manager" simply doesn't exist. All our ground rules—complaining and getting satisfaction ... it's unknown in Russia. And if you don't get satisfaction ... well, you go home. Often, I wanted so much for someone to say that they would have mercy on me! But it didn't happen.　　**(KR)**

My adoption coordinator and his lawyer lined me up with a pregnant birthmother. That apparently was unusual; ordinarily the child has already been born before adoptive parents are notified. The news certainly made me feel really hopeful, but the frustrating thing was that I was never told the birthmother's correct due date. So I waited; it got to be August, September, November. I was just hanging in there. Eventually they said the baby was expected in December. Finally at the end of January, they called to say the baby was born.

All along, I kept thinking, something's wrong. Why aren't they giving me more information? And also, I can't believe I'm putting up with this kind of stalling and excuses. But you know, once you have a baby in the pipeline, you don't want to give up. I felt I had invested so much time and money that I couldn't give up. The adoption coordinator kept demanding things; in November he told me and several other people he was dealing with that he needed $5,000 from each of us to get the process going. We were all taken aback; it was a huge chunk of money! But he told us all that it was the way he worked, and if we wanted the adoptions to go through ... well, we all paid him, somehow.

There's a real lesson in this. If you think something's weird, it's weird. If it seems fishy, it is. I should have stopped right there—but I didn't. When you're doing an adoption at such a distance, what you have is so intangible that you often leap into the void. Yes, you do have to trust ... *but you also have to trust your instinct.*　　**(FS)**

About a week before we were supposed to leave, I ran into a friend. "Did you hear that radio report on Peru last night?" he asked. I hadn't. "It was all about the Shining Path (a terrorist organization that had been devastating Peru for years). They said that they would be celebrating their fifteenth anniversary next month by gunning down tourists. I thought you should know." My heart went right to my mouth; next month was only a week and a half away. As soon as I got home, we called the State Department hotline that advises travelers to other countries. What my friend had said was true; there was a serious travel advisory out for Peru. There's nothing so scary as hearing this somber, dispassionate voice declare that "the United States Department of State warns all travelers to exercise extreme caution . . . " in a country you expect to be in in the next few days. What should we do? We went around and around. Should we delay the trip? Cancel? But the more we considered changing our plans, the more we knew we couldn't. We had made a commitment to our son, and we had to follow through.

(LVP)

Jean's Journal

February 3, 1989

Late last night on the radio, a short news flash: "At 9:00 P.M. Chicago time the thirty-four-year-old government of Alfredo Stroessner of Paraguay fell to a military coup. Cannon and rifle shots have been heard in downtown Asunción, and tanks are in the streets . . . "

I heard it as I drove, but I didn't believe it. We never hear of Paraguay in the news. It must be some mistake, I told myself. Someone confused it with Uruguay (which is never in the news either, of course), or made it up altogether. I slept quite well; such is the power of denial.

But this morning there is no doubt. The adoption agency cannot reach Paraguay by phone. The senator's office is waiting for a State Department advisory. The bishop, who knows clergy throughout South America, is on retreat. There is no word but what I heard last night: "Cannon and rifle shots have been heard . . . tanks are in the streets . . . "

A grim sense of humor seizes me. The radio says Stroessner has been given twelve hours to get out of Paraguay; but where do old Nazis go when they've been thrown out of Paraguay? Ironically, one of the reasons I selected Paraguay was its political stability.

And Ricardo—his soothing voice that has reassured me so often during these last months, a voice I can still hear only three days ago: "We have a referral of a little girl . . . " He was scheduled to arrive in Asunción with his own child and wife sometime yesterday. He was supposed to see you today, to place you in foster care, to send pictures. Where is he?

I am caught between deadly calm and gut-wrenching terror. Will you be safe? Will you get out? Is Ricardo all right? Shall I go to the airport and make my way somehow to Paraguay, I with my halting Spanish, I who have never shot at anything and have never been shot at? Shall I sit here and try to work (let's see now . . . tuition is paid at quarterly intervals . . .), waiting for the phone to ring? Or shall I forget about the child in Paraguay who has, simply by being, already brought me such joy, and start the process again in another far-off country?

Oh, Jessie, are you all right?

February 6

Dear Jessie,

I am up and down all at once. There has been a telegram from Ricardo: "My family and I are safe." Thank God. But what about you? He says nothing about you. Prayers were said for your safety and his yesterday at the cathedral.

This morning the agency says I should think about starting again in another country, "to be prudent." As if the child in Paraguay is so easily set aside. It is incredible to me how bonded one becomes simply to the idea of a child; even Naomi says how close she feels already to you. I have asked if I should just go. I could be ready in a day or two. But the agency says no, that everything is being done that can be. I have set out my suitcase and my passport anyway.

Tonight the news is better. Another woman working with the agency is still planning to leave for Paraguay this Friday. She has called the State Department to ask if it would be safe for her seventy-six-year-old mother to go as well. The person she spoke with said yes, so long as her mother doesn't drink the water.

Dear God! No one told me international adoption would be like this. Or maybe they did. Maybe I just didn't hear it.

February 8

Jessie,

. . . a reprieve! No. More than that. *How quickly can I get to Paraguay?*

Ricardo says he will try to process the four children identified before he left the States—four children, including my little girl, identified twenty-four hours before his departure. He says he will see if it is possible to do any others, but of these he seems confident. I ask how the political situation is. Ricardo says it is 105 degrees—too hot to make a revolution.

I rush around ordering plane tickets and checking on a baby's visa. I am vaguely concerned about continuing political instability. Stroessner is gone, but his son, whose possible succession is said to have triggered the coup, remains in Asunción. There are rumors even now of a countercoup.

And yet, I think that women have always borne some risks to have their children, mostly in their own beds, or in hospitals, true, but risks nonetheless. Perhaps I am foolhardy. Perhaps good sense, caution even, will seize me as I sit in the Miami airport waiting for an overnight flight to Paraguay. Certainly the prospect of this trip has taken on even more of a sense of adventure. Nothing so mundane as a trip to the hospital for me!

Mostly, Jessie, I want you home, safe, where I can see you and touch you. Some people say the sense of completion in the international adoption process comes when you hold your child for the first time. For others, it comes as your plane lands on U.S. soil. For still others, it comes finally when you place your child in her crib for the first time. I wonder when, if ever, it will come for me.

February 10

I lie awake at night now playing out the possible scenarios for this adoption. When I finally drift off, I dream of conversations with my daughter. "Mama . . . why did you name me Jessie?"

Because, love, Jessie and variations of it are traditional names among women on both sides of my family. It seems right, as I face the imminent process of bringing you home to become a member of my family, to give you a name that plants you somehow in the Dutch-American soil from which my own heritage springs.

The first Jessie Knoll was my father's mother. She died before I was born, so all I know about her I have learned from those who knew her. She was, they tell me, strong and intelligent, a self-taught student of the Bible who taught for many years in the Dutch church where my father grew up. I look at her pictures and discover the square jaw and the slightly smaller left eye she gave to my dad, who passed them on to me. I see her intelligence and her character in those pictures, but not much laughter; I know her life was hard, and as I think about it, she is not much remembered for her warmth. Still, everyone remembers her as Mother Knoll.

My favorite story about Jessie happened while she lived with my newly married mother and father. I gather the first Jessie had some fairly definite ideas about things. One of them was about liquor—or, more precisely, about how one should never, ever use liquor. My father and mother, as young adults, fancied themselves quite liberated of their Calvinist background, and so decided to serve liquor at their first Christmas open house. On the night of that party, a deeply troubled Jessie locked herself in her room.

To this party my father invited all the people with whom he worked, including an African American Ph.D. chemist. At first, the doctor declined, saying that he really didn't drink. But my father encouraged him, promising him a soft drink. When the good doctor arrived, he saw that my dad was preoccupied and so made his way instead to the punch bowl. The punch was made of some concoction of fruit juices and liquors that no one who knows anything about alcohol would ever create; but my mother didn't know anything about alcohol and made it from a recipe in a magazine "because it looked so pretty." The chemist had one glass, then another, made some pleasant conversation, and presently prepared to leave. He went out on the icy front porch and, as this dignified gentleman bent over to retrieve his boots, became dizzy and lost his balance. With a loud whoop, he fell backward off the porch into a snow-covered evergreen bush beneath Jessie's bedroom window. And he began to laugh. The harder he tried, and failed, to get a footing in the ice and snow, the harder he laughed. It was everything Jessie had feared about parties where alcohol was served. She didn't speak to my folks for a week.

On my parents' wedding day Jessie gave my mother her most precious possession, a garnet brooch, which she told my mother to save for her daughter, and which I now save for mine. When I was a little girl, I used to study that brooch in its case. For some reason it made me think Jessie liked me. Sometimes I would go with my father to visit his mother's grave, and I'd bring my dollies to show her. I used to think it made Jessie smile to have me playing house in the grass near her gravestone while my father planted flowers. Perhaps when you get home, we'll go there together and find out if we can make her smile again.

Then there was my mother, Jean, although she always went by Winifred or Winnie to avoid confusion with her sister, Jennie. She was the sweetest person anyone who knew her had ever met. Gentle. Demure. Religious. The product of the stern Calvinist upbringing of the midwestern Dutch, like my father. As a girl, she had wanted to become a nurse, but my grandfather insisted on college and conservatory instead. After college she played some piano concerts in and around Chicago, and after one of these she met my dad. And year after year as I grew up, on their wedding anniversary, she sat at the piano in our living room in the long black dress she had worn that night waiting for him, playing Debussy's "Clair de Lune."

We called my mother Our Lady of the Perfect Manners because she was concerned to do everything correctly and thus to avoid offending anyone. One thing she was meticulous about was introductions, of everyone to everyone else. In her last few years, when she was in the hospital for one thing or another, Mother sometimes became confused and proceeded to introduce nurses to nurses' aides, nephews to their aunts and uncles, and me to the preacher who had buried my father. On the morning of the day she died, I was out of town, and while I drove furiously back to Chicago, that preacher, Eddie, went to sit with her for me. When he got there, he told me later, he had stroked her cheek. She had awakened then, smiled, and said, "Oh, look, Eddie, the preacher's here." At the end of that long day, as Eddie and I sat having something to eat, he raised his glass, and with tears in his eyes said, "To your mother, who came full circle today. She went to heaven, and she introduced me to myself."

So sweet and gentle was my mother that most of us hardly knew how strong she was. I saw her strength finally as she died, through two long and painful years of a disease we could not name. And when it was clear that she would not get well, she took the time to talk with everyone she loved, to help us say good-bye to her. She dictated a journal about her life to me, for the grandchildren she would not live long enough to be remembered by. And she arranged the details of her own funeral because she said she knew her children would be upset. All she left for her daughters to do was to select what clothes she would be buried in . . . something nice, she said, and not "a dull, dead color." And she wanted clean underwear, new stockings, and comfortable shoes. When I asked her why on earth comfortable shoes, she looked at me in amazement: "Because at the last judgment, I may have to walk somewhere!" So everyone else will meet at the foot of God's throne in their dull, dead colors and bare feet, but you will know your Grandma Knoll by her pretty aqua-colored suit and scarf and her low-heeled black pumps, Our Lady of the Perfect Manners even in eternity. I have wondered many times in the years since then if I will bring to the end of my life, a life almost totally different from my mother's, a fraction of the dignity and grace with which she ended hers.

I wonder what Jessie and Jean Winifred would think of us: I, divorced and living alone, about to make a little brown baby from the other side of the world my daughter. Startled, I suspect, and certainly disapproving of the divorce that ended my eleven-year marriage. Also sorry for me that while I live a full and productive life, I have so little family with whom to share it. I think they both knew great joy as mothers and so, with time, would finally come to some peace about my wanting to be a mother too. And without a doubt, they would have loved you.

Sometimes in my dreams my mother is here now, watching and waiting with me until I can leave for South America. Naomi, who will serve in her place as your grandma, says that part is no dream.

February 18

The child that was Jessie, the child I thought was Jessie, is no more. The adoption has fallen through.

Two nights ago I staggered home under the weight of baby presents from the shower they had for me at the office. Sweet little stuffed animals and stretchy outfits, little toys and books and rattles. There was so much I could hardly carry it, but it was too precious to me to leave overnight in the office. Besides, I was packing the baby's suitcase so I could leave today, and wanted to bring these things along. So I bought several large shopping bags for all the gifts, then stopped on my way home to buy scented paper to line my baby's dresser drawers.

There were two messages for me on the answering machine when I got home. The first affirmed that the visa documents, rushed through Immigration and Naturalization in time for my scheduled departure for Asunción, had been wired. The second, from the international adoption agency, said they finally had information about the baby. I called Margaret, the social worker, at her home. I couldn't wait, I told her. I still had my coat on.

From her hesitation, I knew something was terribly wrong. The biological mother, nineteen years old, apparently signed the adoption authorization papers when she entered the hospital some six weeks ago. She said then that she didn't expect to be coming home, and she wanted to be sure her baby was cared for. But now she is home and feeling stronger. And she wants to keep her baby. Margaret said I could wait a few days to see if the mother changes her mind again, but I said no. That young mother has a right to her child that I do not, no matter how desperately I may want her; and she has the right to have this decision, and its unmaking, made as easy and as unpressured for her as possible. I could not live with the thought that any child I adopt may be pressured or seduced, unwillingly, from the mother who bore her.

I sat alone in the dark stillness for a long time after I hung up, wrapped in a sense of profound aloneness. At first I did not cry.

Somehow, in a way I cannot explain, I had a child. I never held her or touched her or had a picture of her. I never even heard her cry. But I saw her in her crib upstairs, her black hair against the eyelet comforter. I sat in her room and rocked peacefully each night, listening to the music box in her mobile. I awoke in the morning and wondered how many more mornings I would sleep that late, the cats curled on the pillows beside me.

And *that* Jessie is no more.

Yes, of course, there are other babies and other lists and even other agencies. There is more money in the bank. This is not the end, I tell myself, only a brief detour. I can rearrange the maternity leave and the airline tickets when another baby is referred to me. This child was not, after all, *my* Jessie, but someone else.

I tell myself the grief I feel is irrational, stupid, unnecessary. But my heart tells me I have lost a child. I feel how powerfully that unknown, unheld child had already taken hold of my life, and of the lives of people who would have been her family . . . all the more powerfully perhaps because she was still in many ways unreal to us. My heart tells me that *that* Jessie has somehow died.

I wish to God I could be angry with someone! But there is something so clearly right about that nineteen-year-old girl's desire to keep her child that I find it impossible to be angry, even at God. What I feel instead is simply emptiness, and the insistent fear that nothing I can ever do will give me back the family I so long to have again. And remarkably, I feel embarrassed, even a little ashamed, that I should have been so giddily happy, and that I should have caught up in that happiness so many people who care about me. I feel as though I have used them somehow, taken advantage of their good offices on my behalf, and have been the source, however unwittingly, of pain they did not deserve.

And how will I tell Naomi and Lonnie? Naomi, making a christening gown fit for a princess. Lonnie, who cannot walk past a toy store these past few weeks without stopping to look in the window. How can I protect them? Will they, or any of the other people who shared my joy, ever want to be a part of this again? Will they dare?

I was reading a book earlier this week about parent-child bonding. I skimmed the chapter at the end detachedly, the one about losing a baby at birth. It said that people don't know what to say when grief and loss rush into the place that was supposed to have been filled by the joy of birth and new life. It described people who say to the parents of a stillborn child, "Well, you can get pregnant again," and "The baby probably wouldn't have been right," and "This is for the best." The few people I have been able to tell haven't known very well what to say to me either. They say they are not surprised, if the baby had been in her family three months already. They ask me if this kind of thing happens often, as if I knew. They ask if I'll get my money back. I understand that these people who love me, and by extension already loved this child, speak out of shock and surprise, as if the flow of their emotions has been suddenly wrenched in some new and unexpected direction. I hear their pain because I know my own. A very few respond in ways that give comfort. Peggy, of course, by saying nothing: she choked with tears, whispered that she could not bear such pain for me, and then hung up the phone. And Phyllis too, who was simply silent, letting the phone line connect us.

A few weeks ago, right after the coup in Paraguay, another woman who is thinking about adoption called me. She said she had had three failed pregnancies, and that she had hoped through adoption to get off her emotional merry-go-round. Maybe this is just the beginning of that merry-go-round for me. Maybe I should have listened more carefully to all my fears at the beginning. Maybe there will never be a Jessie Victoria Knoll after all. Maybe I do not have the courage for it.

February 23

I spoke today with another single woman who has adopted a little girl from Chile. She called me to tell me that she knew how this was, that she, too, had had a child referred to her who was ultimately reassigned to a two-parent family. She says she was so angry that she took no time to mourn that loss and rushed headlong into another referral, mercifully a successful one. Even now, years later, she says she still dreams that one day the agency calls her to say that the first child is waiting for her, but they do not tell her where.

And so, reluctantly, I called the international adoption agency today to ask that they take my name off their waiting list for a little while. I explained to them that I need some time to heal, some time to prepare myself for dealing with other referrals, all of them inevitably shadowed from now on with the knowledge of what could go wrong. Margaret was sympathetic and asked me to let her know when I was ready.

An hour later, John, the adoption agency manager, called me. He was plainly annoyed, even a little angry. He said this would not look good to the local judges in Paraguay, that they would think I did not really want to be a mother, that other parents' cases could be jeopardized by my "poor showing." He asked me to think about it overnight.

And so in the middle of this sleepless night, I wonder what I have done. Am I indeed so emotionally self-indulgent that I am willing to hurt not only my own chances of adopting but those of other parents as well? Are a few future bad dreams worth risking so much? Or is this not really much about me, but about the business the agency is running? I am beginning to suspect that my feelings are somewhat less important to them just now than their record of placements.

But . . . how do I know?

March 4

The agency called me yesterday—was I ready to get back on the waiting list? I cannot answer them.

Some part of me jumps at the hope of it. Another child, perhaps soon. More plans and hopes, more looking forward instead of back. Gain and not loss. Birth and not death. A woman in the women's group who also lost a referral has called. She says she threw herself back into the search process immediately and that in a few months she had another child. I have barely even spoken to this woman, and I am so touched by her willingness to describe her own painful loss and hard-won joy to someone she hardly knows.

Yet some part of me pulls back, as if the grief isn't done yet. The other would-be mother says she never let herself mourn. She still has the picture of her first child, still imagines the agency might one day call her and tell her the child is waiting for her. She says the fear that she might lose the child she adopted shortly after her referral fell through shadowed her first weeks and months with her new daughter. As if the good-byes had never properly been said, and as if God would yet require some proper leave-taking.

So, though I don't fully understand it myself, I have given this grief its space. Several days alone and quiet, without even the phone or the television. Several quiet days just being alone with this sadness and sense of loss. I slept till I woke, then read and wrote and cried till I slept again. In those days I forced myself to reread this journal, to edit its chapters. It reminded me of all that had brought me so long ago to this decision. It brought back the hopes and the doubts that have run like a thread through it from the beginning. And I realize, after many readings, that this story is somehow not finished.

Two chapters seem possible now. One, that I decide I cannot do this again. I feel like a ball at the end of a rubber band on one of those wooden paddles I played with as a girl. Bouncing forward and backward, up and down. How long, I wonder, before the rubber band finally snaps? The other chapter tells that I try again, in spite of knowing what can happen. It was easier to be courageous when I could not imagine all the possibilities.

However the story continues, I know now I must finish saying good-bye to this child who will never come. Like a child stillborn, there is no body, no ceremony. I started to throw the agency's final bill away, then realized it is all that I have to show that the child I loved for sixteen days ever really existed. For the last two weeks I haven't been able to go into the baby's room whose door I have locked. Today, I began to put away the things in the nursery—the little stretchy outfits and sweaters, the teddy bear, the gifts from the shower on the day I got the phone call—in boxes and bags for the basement and closet. I have made several appointments with my priest and friend Tony, as a time set aside to finish this grief, whatever else happens.

It begins to seem that in time I will engage this process again, though I can't say exactly when. I will be more cautious then about my joy. I will admit it to my life gradually, the way the sun moves across my yard in the early morning. I will keep it to myself and tell only a few people when I must. I have learned a new kind of grief, not the wracking, raging sadness tinged with anger that I have known before but a pain so deep that words and even tears have expressed it only partially. One day, if and when I reopen the boxes of baby clothes, what I know from this grief will add to a joy paid for so dearly. Eventually, there will be perhaps an even better celebration of the coming of the child called Jessie because it has been so deferred. But the deepest part of the joy will be mine, only mine, lying beside a sadness that women who have lost a child do not forget.

March 20

Almost a month has elapsed since my last contact with the adoption agency. I know I have taken a terrible risk to ask that my name be taken off the agency's referral list for this long. I know that it is possible that someone in Michigan or someone in Paraguay has already decided not to refer another child to me. But I also know that if I do not take care of my own feelings in this, who will?

I wonder what this process does to two-parent relationships. My grief has felt so deep and so personal that I doubt I could have shared it with anyone. And if two people grieve so, their unspoken grief would surely separate them, pull them apart. And then they would have that to mourn for too, for the loss of intimacy between them, for the support they could not give each other. Though I hope for another such relationship in my life one day, maybe hard as this is, doing it alone is easier.

I have needed some kind of ceremony to help me say a final good-bye to the child that might have been Jessie. Something like a funeral, I suppose. So last weekend I made the long drive to the cemetery where my grandmother Jessie is buried. I hiked through the snow drifts for a long time until at last I found the stone that read "Jessie Knoll." I left flowers there, yellow mums, lying on the white snow.

And almost miraculously, in the days since that visit the old excitement of anticipation has begun again at the thought of another referral. A sign, I suppose, that healing has occurred. Am I ready for the uncertainty that will come with reactivating? I'm not sure, but I guess I will never know without trying.

I will call Margaret in the morning.

April 1

Dear Jessie,
(yes, I dare to write to you again)

Today the agency in Michigan has called to tell me about a newborn child who has been surrendered to foster care. They say she seems well, and was born in a hospital in Asunción after an apparently normal pregnancy. Would I like this referral? I ask a few questions, but I am surprised at how willingly I say yes. If all goes well, I can leave for Paraguay in three to four weeks.

But how differently I am behaving this time! I have told one or two people and have made another appointment with my dean to negotiate a maternity leave. Past experience has taught me that an adoptive maternity leave is not easy to arrange, so I must allow as much planning time as possible. Maternity leave, it seems, is customarily paid for out of short-term disability funds, and it seems clear that I will not be disabled. So some patchwork of unused vacation, personal leave, and sick days must be assembled to allow me up to six weeks of paid leave. After that, I am on my own. I vaguely remember meeting a woman at a support group for single adoptive parents who said that when she returned from South America, she was so exhausted and weak from intestinal infections that her own physician requested a short-term medical leave for her, which allowed her some time to get settled with her little one. It is an option to keep in mind, I suppose, though not a very appealing one.

Emotionally, I hold myself in check. Though I long to reopen the nursery and look again at the sweet little shower presents still in their boxes, I cannot, not yet. Though I should call the travel agent as soon as possible, I will not, not yet. Not till this seems more real. But, deep inside, oh, how I want *this* one to be real!

April 18

This morning I sent a check for another set of plane tickets to Paraguay. This afternoon, the agency called to tell me that the baby girl referred to me has syphilis. I am disappointed, but not surprised this time. And I am overwhelmingly sorry for the child.

I asked how long another referral might take. Margaret says she thinks the lawyer has another baby about to be born, and that she will call me back in a day or so.

The night before last, I reopened up the nursery. Tonight, I have closed it again. The waiting, the hoping, the fear that this may never work out, go on.

April 24

I have thought so often of the baby girl in Paraguay over these past few days. I have asked Wong about the possible effects of infant syphilis. He says they vary according to how early the infection was contracted. Damage can be minimal if the infection did not occur until the child entered the birth canal. But if contracted in utero, the damage can be dreadful: blindness, retardation, seizure disorder, heart defects. And there is no way of discerning when a newborn contracted the disease. All that can be done is to give her a course of antibiotics to kill the infection that is active now.

After I talked to Wong, I found myself wondering if an abandoned child in the Third World can even be assured of that course of antibiotics. It would not cost much for me to pay for that. So this morning I called Margaret. Before I could make my offer, Margaret told me it was all a mistake, a "false positive," and that the baby is fine after all. I can leave any time, she said. When I hesitated, she said that what she would do is go to Paraguay, take custody of the baby, and have her completely examined and tested again by a physician of my own choosing; then, if I didn't like the results, I could give her back.

Immediately, I called Wong who told me what I suspected: that even an infected baby would test negative after a course of antibiotics, and that there is now no way of telling if the infection had ever been present in her. He said the kind of damage that can be done by in utero syphilis may well not be detectable immediately. Finally, he reminded me of the economics of poverty, and of the incentives to pass off as healthy a child who is not.

I called Margaret back and declined the referral. I said I would not take this risk. I told her I had nursed my own mother as she died; that I had held her in my arms during the seizures she suffered at the end of her life; that I know from real experience what it means to watch those we love suffer. Margaret was very irritated. She said that even a biological child of my own would have health risks. I assured her that one of them would not be syphilis.

Shortly afterward, John called. He was plainly angry that I was once again demonstrating my lack of desire to become a parent. I pointed out to him that becoming the single parent of a healthy infant will be challenging enough, and that under the circumstances, caution seems prudent. I said I had signed an agreement with his agency to locate, insofar as this could be determined, a "healthy infant," and that the health of this particular infant seems dubious at best. He asked me if my decision was firm. I said it was.

Tonight, of course, the clarity and firmness of broad daylight have disappeared. I so admire those parents who decide to adopt a child with "special needs," and I think I could probably manage it too, if I had to. But I also know that the admiration of others for such caring, which in the past I have given willingly and with all my heart, was poor comfort as I held my mother in the middle of the night. If I adopt an apparently healthy child who then becomes ill, of course I would care for her. But don't I have a right not to ask for this?

On the other hand, maybe this child would have been all right. Maybe my caution is another manifestation of my early fears. Maybe the agency will never call me again.

April 25

Late this evening my phone rang. A woman introduced herself as a physician who sometimes works with the Michigan adoption agency. She said John had asked her to call me to reassure me about the health of the child who has been referred to me. She said American physicians know so little about Third-World disease and are therefore so "conservative" in their recommendations; I pointed out to her that the physician I have been consulting was trained in Singapore. She continued to urge me to reconsider; Third-World adoptions, she said, are always risky.

What I am learning, painfully, is that international adoption agencies are of two kinds. The first are those staffed by trained social workers who understand and respect the emotional dimensions of this process. The second are those that are staffed (if we are lucky) by well-intentioned and honest laypeople who function as little more than links between adoptive parents and someone in a far-off country who locates available children. Even though these agencies must know how desperately people who seek adoptions overseas want children, even though they must know how difficult refusing a referral would be for us, for them this is a business. In spite of knowing the emotional costs adoptive parents pay, perhaps even *because* they know these costs, the agency in Michigan apparently is not above playing on my vulnerability to complete their "transaction" with me. I am startled to realize that no agency of all that I've talked to has given me a definition of a "healthy" child. I wonder if they will even tell the next people to whom they offer this child about the "false positive."

It is finally time for me to be angry. I will call my lawyer in the morning.

May 15

Today I saw my wonderful social worker, Julie. It seems the agency in Michigan has told her that I am "unstable," and while her support for me has been unwavering from the beginning, she is professionally obligated to investigate this charge. So today I made the long drive to her office, carrying a written assessment of my emotional status from a clinical social worker. It assures her agency that I am understandably angry but otherwise quite fine, and that there is no chance that John's allegation that I might abandon a less-than-perfect child is true. I am also carrying a card from my lawyer.

We had a good talk, I cried a little, and then Julie and I talked about what to do next. I told her I was not especially anxious to try another adoption agency after this experience, and that my inclination now is to work directly with an attorney in Paraguay. She has given me the name of a woman who successfully adopted an infant girl last Christmas using a Paraguayan attorney. Then she gave me a hug and told me she knew I'd be a wonderful mother. I hope one day she knows what that hug meant to me.

May 27

Dear Doctor G:

I thought that I would write to you in English because I am afraid that my halting Spanish is somewhat inadequate for this complicated and painful subject. Because of Sharon's confidence in you, and her respect for you, I feel that I can tell you honestly how difficult this adoption process has been so far.

As I told you on the telephone, I have lost the referral of two baby girls (and a third that was promised) within the last two months. I do not believe that the adoption agency with whom I have worked is dishonest or disreputable, but I am afraid that they have so many people who want to adopt children that they do not give much care to any single application. Based on their referrals and promises, I have arranged with my superiors and colleagues at the university to have my teaching responsibilities excused for a total of nine months. If I do not take this leave of absence very soon, I may be unable to arrange any further time away from my responsibilities for a long time.

I would like to adopt a healthy baby girl, as young as possible. As an unmarried woman, I feel better able to raise a little girl in my society than I do a little boy. As a professor, I earn a comfortable salary, and my parents (who are deceased) have left me with enough money to provide well for a child. I live in a big house near the university, with a nice garden where a child could play safely. There are many people in my life who support my decision to adopt as a single parent and who will act in the place of a more traditional family.

Sharon and her baby are coming to my home for dinner later this week. I am anxious to see Katherine as she grows up, and Sharon and I both hope that soon her daughter will have a little girlfriend from Paraguay here in the United States. When I tell Sharon that sometimes I am afraid I may never receive my little girl, and may never be able to name a child after my grandmother, Jessie Victoria, she always tells me to trust Dr. G. She says I will be proud to have you represent me, and that I should be full of hope.

I look forward to hearing from you.

Sincerely,
Jean Knoll

August 1

The long wait continues . . .

I speak with my lawyer in Paraguay every two weeks or so. He always says he is hopeful of something soon. I have sent him a check, which he says he will not cash until he has located a child.

I believe Sharon, the woman who worked with him last Christmas, when she says that Dr. G is an honorable man. I *must* believe her. I know that I could not deal with the adoption agency in Michigan any more, or frankly with any other agency just now.

But in my darkest moments, I fear that John and Margaret have somehow found Dr. G and have shared with him their opinion that I am unstable and uncommitted to parenthood. Late at night, I imagine Dr. G too steeped in Hispanic gallantry to say this to me, but with too much integrity to place a child in my care. Even too much integrity to take my money.

And later at night, I wonder if I can go on with this process much longer.

September 5

Paraguay has closed.

Today I called Dr. G once again: "How is it going? Is there any word?" And today he explained the slowness of the summer. He has seen this coming. The new government has dissolved the judiciary. No new adoption cases can begin, and those that have been started are suspended. Families have been stranded in Paraguay, or have had to give up their adoptive children and come home.

God bless Dr. G for saving me at least this. God damn him for delivering such news. I called Julie, and she confirmed the news. She has advised all the families with whom she works to give up on Paraguay.

Dr. G said there will be no adoptions now until after the holidays, which go on in Paraguay well into January. He said that when the courts reopen, the rules may be very different: longer waiting periods, higher fees, even different eligibility requirements. I asked him if he thought that single-parent adoptions might be disallowed; he said he doubted this, but it is possible.

After I hung up the phone, I cried and screamed like a two-year-old having a temper tantrum.

September 30

I have made a few lackadaisical phone calls to new adoption agencies. They have sent me materials about their programs. I look at the long list of documents: another copy of the homestudy, another set of essays, another police clearance, another financial report . . .

I'm not sure I can face starting from scratch again, putting all of these documents together for another long and frustrating process. My rising and falling hopes have left me emotionally exhausted, and a little numb. So many times I have heard that in contrast to the biological process, there is always a child somewhere in the world at the end of the international adoption process. I have wondered, given the eventual certainty of the outcome, why many people do not finally complete an adoption this way.

And now I know. They simply wear out.

November 17

Asunción, Paraguay

The Honorable AJD
United States Senate
230 South Dearborn
Chicago, Illinois 60604

Dear Senator D:

This letter is in response to your recent inquiry into the status of the adoption case of your constituent, Ms. Jean W. Knoll.

For years, Americans have been legally adopting Paraguayan children in accordance with United States and Paraguayan law. However, on August 29, the Paraguayan supreme court issued an accord suspending adoption of Paraguayan children by persons living outside of Paraguay. The publication of this accord appears to have ended a two-month period in which the government of Paraguay attempted to come to grips with rapidly increasing numbers of adoptions from abroad. Since mid-June, the judiciary, in anticipation of a change, had stalled adoptions by those living abroad. Article four (4) of this document, however, called for the "normal" processing of those cases already in adjudication.

The embassy has conducted a series of ambassadorial and consular interventions at all levels of government on behalf of families already in Asunción. Unfortunately families that arrived since mid-June have not been allowed to proceed with their adoptions. Despite the provisions of Article 4 noted above, the cases have not proceeded smoothly.

The emotional and financial price exacted from those families already here has been substantial. Given the fluid nature of this issue we have recommended that additional families whose cases are still in adjudication not, repeat not, come to Asunción until the situation has stabilized. Even though the Knoll family has not yet arrived in Asunción, please rest assured that once they do, we will monitor the progress of their case and provide assistance when needed.

Thank you for your interest in the Knoll case. Should you have any further questions or comments, please do not hesitate to write or call.

Sincerely yours,
Clarence H
Consular Section

December 23

Last year at this time, as I turned forty, I told my friends I would celebrate the arrival of my middle age by having a baby. Today, I turn a childless forty-one.

Last Christmas I put up a second Christmas tree for my baby. This year, there is only one tree, and the porcelain baby bootie ornament is put away. No one at the tree-trimming party had the indelicacy to mention it. Last year, there was a stocking hanging by the fireplace with Jessie's name on it. This year, the only stockings contain treats for the cats. Last year, people's Christmas presents to me included things for a baby's nursery. This year, the nursery, closed up for so long, has finally been dismantled; the Portacrib and the rocker and the baby shower gifts are all carefully wrapped and stored in the basement.

After a year and a half of waiting, perhaps it is time to accept that God, or someone, has said no. I have given this process everything I had for so long, draining love and support from all the people who care about me, to no avail. I am tired and discouraged and demoralized. I look at mothers with their children in the grocery store and on the train, and I think I would have been as good a mother as they.

Yet some little piece of me still holds on. The baby things, though stored away, could be brought back in an instant. The sofa bed I ordered, to turn the nursery into a TV room, I canceled. I even tried to sell the house once and buy a high-rise condominium, but I couldn't go through with it. Because one day, what if the phone rings and Dr. G's voice asks me how soon I can get to Paraguay? I still, intermittently, keep this journal.

Oh, Jean, get a life! . . . not the one you wanted maybe, but a life nonetheless.

February 1, 1990

I called Paraguay today. Nothing has changed. I don't talk about adoption much anymore with anyone except Dr. G.

March 10

I talked to Dr. G today. The adoption courts are still closed in Paraguay. I am past the point of crying after these phone calls.

April 15

Nothing is new in Paraguay. I didn't have a little girl as a tax deduction after all.

June 6

I called Dr. G again today. With great sadness, he told me once again that nothing has changed. He says he has expected movement for months, and now that there has been none, he no longer knows what to tell me. Of course, I should hold on if I like. Certainly adoptions will happen again in Paraguay . . . someday. I am still at the top of his list.

As I always do, I called Julie to verify what I am being told. And yes, all of her parents are going somewhere else to adopt. Then, I heard papers rustling on her desk. Somewhere, she said, she had a postcard from an international relief organization. It said they have a new adoption program, operating in the out-of-the-way places where they do their other work. Perhaps they would have some ideas for me. I wrote the phone number down on a little piece of paper and taped it to the lamp on my desk. These days it is often only Julie's continued, unwavering support of me that keeps even tenuous hope alive.

However this process finally ends, how will I ever thank her?

"Up and Down
All at Once"

commentary

Adoption stories often come with warnings attached; sadly, Jean's story is a case in point. But is it fair to say that any attempt to adopt is fraught with difficulty? Is it possible that each of the more than 7,300 international adoptions and estimated 115,000 domestic adoptions completed in the United States in 1993 were problematic in some way?

Due to recent highly publicized stories that detail the difficulties some adopters have experienced in the course of domestic adoption, some prospective adoptive parents have made the assumption that intercountry adoption might be just the way to avoid any potential custody disputes or court battles. But, as in any domestic adoption, there is always the possibility that something will go wrong during an intercountry adoption. Though problems between birthparents and adoptive parents rarely occur during carefully supervised agency or independent adoptions, problems of a different nature can surface.

This is due in part to the number of parties involved in intercountry adoption. At the very least, there are three primary participants: adopter, child, and birthparent. But in most cases, you must also add adoption agency staff, adoption coordinator, foreign adoption program workers, lawyer, translator, a number of foreign government employees ranging from lowly paper pushers to judges, and finally U.S. Immigration and Naturalization Service (INS) officials. With such a huge cast of characters, it's easy to see that the intercountry adoption process isn't likely to move quickly and easily. In fact, the majority of problems most parents agonize over in an international adoption have to do with an unexpected lengthy wait at some point during the process.

Adoption proceedings can stretch out for several reasons: glitches in paperwork and/or documentation required by the United States and the foreign country; the current adoption backlog (significant in large foreign cities); how much local bureaucracy is involved in processing the adoption overseas; and the country's current political scene. "The thing about it," says one parent who waited six months before her child came home, "is that the adoption will happen, but the thing that probably won't happen is the time frame. The waiting was horrible for me back then. But I guess I'd say now that I was fulfilling a dream by adopting my child, and dreams are supposed to take a long time."

This is an extremely forgiving viewpoint. Most people would agree that the disruption of their lives for several months put a strain on their home and work life, and made a significant dent in the savings that were meant to sustain the very child whose adoption has caused such upset.

Much of the waiting adopters experience during an intercountry adoption is due to human error in some form—an overzealous government official, a lost file, a cultural misunderstanding. But in other cases, there has been the direct problem of foreign governments' worry over their active intercountry adoption programs. The implication is that the country cannot care for its own—an extremely unwelcome image that has caused governments to close their doors abruptly to adopters. This occurred several years ago in South Korea. During the 1988 Olympics Games in Seoul, television segments and newspaper stories here and abroad detailed Korea's dominant role in intercountry adoption: due to poverty and to social taboos against bearing and raising out-of-wedlock infants, thousands of children per year—close to six thousand in 1987 alone—were relinquished by Korean birthparents and adopted by U.S. citizens. This was new information for millions of television viewers, and the publicity angered and embarrassed the South Korean government, which subsequently shut down all adoption activity while it evaluated the situation. Ecuador severely limited international adoption in 1989 after uncovering a kidnapping/adoption ring operating in the province of Pichincha. In 1990 after the breakdown of the Romanian government and the discovery of huge numbers of children languishing under state care, scores of foreigners descended on Bucharest intent on adopting Romanian children. The illegal and unethical arrangements some adopters chose to pursue caused a scandal that closed doors to Romanian adoption in the summer of 1991. Other countries—Russia, for example, have opened, then shut, then opened their doors again to intercountry adoption in the past couple of years. Eastern European countries have typically never had intercountry adoption laws in place; in the rush to open up to the West following the collapse of Communist governments, these countries have had to take a quick step back and close adoptions until international adoption can be properly regulated. "And," says an adoption agency official, "no one wants to be seen as another Romania."

In Peru, the desperate condition of thousands of poor children has provoked a national sense of embarrassment, outrage, and guilt throughout the last ten years. Stories about the foreigners who have come by the thousands to adopt these children have provoked a bitter nationalism, in which the Peruvian press expresses outrage over those who would take advantage of a struggling country by spiriting away its children. It's no wonder that Peru has joined the ranks of countries that are restricting and restructuring international adoption.

The larger international political scene is also responsible for disruption of intercountry adoption. It was the 1989 coup in Paraguay that shut down the government, including the courts through which intercountry adoptions are processed. Vietnam is another case in point: adoptions from there have been very difficult for Americans due to the United States' long-standing embargo on all trade and diplomatic relations following the Vietnam War. Now that the United States has lifted the trade embargo, normal relations will likely be restored in the next few years, making intercountry adoption from Vietnam easier. In countries such as Haiti, where small numbers of children have been adopted by U.S. parents over the past few years, political strife has made adoption agencies move with great caution; waiting children suffer the consequences. The battlegrounds of Eastern Europe have orphaned thousands of children, but there will be no solutions for them until enemies agree to attend to the needs of these innocent victims. Even if thousands of adoptive families wait for such children, political wrangling always seems to take precedence over the needs of the powerless.

How baffling when the intensely personal process of adoption is so upset by the highly impersonal issues of national and international politics! We Americans, who are used to a certain political stability, find this bewildering, frightening, and enormously frustrating, especially if we've pursued intercountry adoption because we hoped it would be a relatively fast process. Our Ugly American impatience is a reflection of our good fortune in being citizens of a powerful nation where government has the resources to be generally responsive to the needs of its people. But if we're angered by foreign governments that are in too much turmoil to deal in an organized way with adoptions, we've missed the point: it is because so many developing countries don't have the resources to function effectively that so many children are available for us to adopt.

Immigration and Naturalization Service statistics that show how many immigrant orphans have been adopted by U.S. citizens give a good indication of which countries are lacking in resources for their citizens. In 1993, Latin America—Mexico, Central and South America, and the Caribbean—accounted for more than 2,500 intercountry adoptions. More than 1,700 children came from Korea, 350 each came from the Philippines and from India. Eastern Europe accounted for over 1,500 children. Circumstances in all these countries vary; their economic instability is due to a great number of historical and political factors that—especially for Asian and Latin American countries—converge in a poverty so deeply rooted that such countries can't refuse the solution of international adoption for some of their children, no matter how desperately governments continue to search for answers to long-standing problems.

As a North American, I'm typically ignorant of economic systems outside my own country. But since the adoption of my daughter, I continue to be fascinated by the way her country's economy has developed and continues to evolve along with its Latin American neighbors. A description of this area of the world is a good example of the multilayered problems so many Third-World countries face; even if its precise situation is different from Eastern Europe's or Asia's, the interrelation of social and economic factors is the same the world over.

The poorer countries of Latin America, though rich in natural and human resources, can't care for their poor because of faltering economic systems born of colonial dependence and exploitation. Recent intervention in poorer Latin American countries in the form of loans and aid from the developed world is responsible for some growth but hasn't fostered economic independence.

There is a long history of exploitation of Central and South America, starting with the Spanish conquests of the 1500s and continuing into the colonial period, which generally ended by the late 1800s. Carrying on into the twentieth century, many developed countries have continued to sap Latin America's natural and human resources, with minimal compensation, rebuilding, and replacement. Internal political disruption and corruption brought on by faulty economies and rising discontent has been encouraged or ignored by outside world powers—including the United States—looking to expand their worldwide sphere of influence. Latin American nations such as Chile, Colombia, and Peru have seen serious political upheaval within the last fifty years, with little resolution of social and economic problems. In present times, poor South American nations struggle with increasing debt and scramble to keep pace with a world marketplace that often demands the exploitation of precious natural resources such as rain forest timber, depleting the few remaining natural assets of these countries. (Ironically, the developed world has now realized that past and present ravages of the Latin American environment are causing serious global climatic problems. But with economies tied to the exploitation of the rain forest, it's no wonder that Latin American countries are angered by our demands that they suddenly become environmentally conscious, no matter what the economic consequences.)

While the exploitation of Latin American lands has resulted in the loss of unique environments, there are other devastating results: countries are suffering the loss of a culture. Rural native Indian populations, often powerless in the face of commercial developers or wealthy landlords, are disappearing. These indigenous peoples have lost their lands and their livelihood to development. They can no longer live self-sufficiently and are therefore at the economic mercy of landowners who recruit them as laborers but barely pay them a living wage. Some groups of indigenous peoples have organized politically in recent years to fight the injustices they have suffered, but their losses continue to mount. In land disputes, or in the seizure of protected lands officially reserved for indigenous peoples, landowners are usually backed by the military and rarely lose. Protests by Indian communities have lead to mass arrests, destruction of property, and death.

The rural communities of Paraguay, Brazil, Chile, Peru, Guatemala, Colombia, and other countries have broken apart under the pressure of development. Those who remain in the countryside face starvation and terrorism. But those who scatter to the cities face a different kind of nightmare: they enter a world of rampant discrimination, where brown skin dooms them to a lower-class invisibility and the poverty and slum existence that accompanies it. The stress these people suffer destroys kinship and guarantees that age-old interdependency and cultural roots will disappear.

People lose land and roots through development; people lose land and roots to drugs. In Peru, Colombia, Brazil, Bolivia, and other Latin American countries, leaders in the booming worldwide narcotics industry have encouraged large-scale cultivation not of traditional food crops but of coca, the raw material needed for cocaine and therefore a lucrative cash crop. Farmers and laborers make money; but they often pay dearly for their part in a narcotics network. Brutal infighting between drug traders can engulf villages in fire, torture, and death. The internationally funded "war on drugs" has given government and paramilitary forces license to destroy homes and crops and terrorize workers. Political opposition groups looking to finance their own operations seize coca harvests and execute witnesses or anyone else who might look like a government sympathizer. Once again, communities are isolated and broken; and once again, the cities beckon.

Millions who flee to urban centers find themselves living in shantytowns: the *barrios* of São Paulo, Medillín, Lima, La Paz. In the last few years, urban populations have swelled—in some cases, doubled—due to such influx. Governments have few resources for dealing with so many in need, and the rift between rich and poor grows wider. Terrorist groups rallying for political change have sprung up, bombing government offices and power plants and killing officials. The military retaliates with equal ferocity. More recently, drug-related fighting from the countryside has moved into the cities, provoking even more violence. People find themselves caught in a crossfire, unable to return to their rural homes but just barely surviving by staying put.

With no money, no jobs, no help from the government, no protection from terrorism, and the bare minimum of shelter and health care, the poor of Latin America have become even poorer and more desperate in the last quarter century. The number of children born to impoverished families has skyrocketed, creating an overwhelming population of orphaned and homeless children. Since most Latin American people come from a tradition of large families and Catholic beliefs, family planning—even if available—isn't an option.

Under these circumstances, children continue to be born, given what little their parents can find for them, are abandoned, and die or are sometimes relinquished for adoption. So often they are not the "unwanted children" that newspapers and magazines talk about; they are indeed wanted, but by parents who find themselves suspended in a hopeless world of poverty and violence where they have lost control to care for themselves, much less their children. In some cases, when one additional hungry mouth could simply push a family over the edge, choosing adoption for a newborn child means that parents can continue to provide for older siblings.

A common cynical viewpoint is that wealthy foreign adoptive parents, faced with increasing infertility and a growing shortage of available adoptive children, are once again using Third-World turmoil to their advantage. It's said that developed nations are continuing the tradition of stripping Latin America of valuable natural resources, but now those resources are human ones: we're adopting away children. It's proposed that intercountry adoption be halted and money instead be channeled directly to poor families so that they can stay together. This is an admirable idea, but it doesn't begin to provide a solution to the complex problems facing the poor of Latin America, or other impoverished areas of the world. Families need more than short-term relief—they need guarantees that they'll actually be alive and able to provide for their children not just now, but ten years from now. Until that can be promised, intercountry adoption is here to stay, because it does guarantee a future for at least some children whose families have so few options. And until the developed world can successfully work alongside Third-World governments to stimulate local economies, eliminate the international narcotics industry, and end corruption and terrorism within and outside the government, there will always be few options for families in need.

It's a sad situation when a government can't provide the necessary care for its citizens. And even if it means great happiness for adoptive parents and new life for adoptees, separating a child from his birthfamily and culture is truly regrettable. Therefore, it's deplorable when international adoption is used by some as a money-making opportunity, reducing a sad but positive situation into nothing more than a bitter transaction. No one is immune to this abuse, neither the birthparents who may be coerced into relinquishing a child nor the adoptive parent who is recruited by a slick operator. In nearly all cases the reason for such abuse is rooted in the amount of money to be made from "wealthy" foreign adoptive parents.

Adopters can be taken advantage of especially by independent contacts and sometimes by adoption agencies. Impatient prospective parents looking to do a cheap quick independent adoption can be unlucky contracting with independent adoption coordinators or foreign lawyers without carefully checking references. Unfortunately, independent contacts made by word of mouth are not always reliable, even if they are recommended by friends or acquaintances who have already successfully adopted through the contact. Even if such contacts are reputable and result in successful adoptions, there are a significant number of disappointments—bungled documents, broken promises, nonexistent children or children made available through frightening illegal arrangements, and extortion of thousands of dollars from families devastated by individuals far away in another country who won't return phone calls or funds. When there is no adoption agency to intervene and attempt to straighten out a bad situation, money is gone and time is wasted, along with hopes for a child and trust in any future intercountry adoption contact. "Even if we do get our money back, how could I trust anyone again?" asked one prospective adoptive parent.

Still, given the right contacts, independent foreign adoptions do work. Since adopting our daughter and getting to know a few parents who worked directly with lawyers in foreign countries, I've sometimes wondered if we, too, couldn't have found Cristina without the help of an agency. But we were like lots of prospective adoptive parents. We wanted the protection of going through an agency, of working with professionals who knew the ropes. We wanted to be sure that we were dealing with people who weren't motivated primarily by finances, and we certainly hoped a child welfare organization such as an adoption agency would be trustworthy and respectful of the amount of money we would invest in the process. And if the truth be known, the biggest reason for going with an adoption agency was that we simply weren't brave enough to do it all on our own.

Licensed agencies employ honest, hard-working administrators and social workers, and the best ones belong to professional groups such as the Joint Council on International Children's Services from North America. All good agencies should and do provide potential adoptive parents with detailed information about their current intercountry adoption programs, contact with families who have adopted through them, and a breakdown of all fees related to an adoption. If an agency is reluctant to supply any of this information, there's something wrong.

Adoption agencies these days are under great financial pressure. Required overseas costs have risen. So has agency overhead: since the international adoption process for many countries has become more complex, staff must spend far more time with each adoptive family before an adoption is completed. Most good agencies continue to upgrade their postadoption services with counseling, workshops, and advocacy, which requires even more staff hours. And there is competition from independent adoption coordinators, who cost less because they don't provide postadoption or other such agency services. Agencies find that besides advocating for the children and families they serve, they must also spend precious energy agonizing over their bottom line.

Skimping on services to make more of a profit would go against the self-regulating code of ethics most child-centered organizations hold to. A good agency stands firmly behind the principle of providing "families for children, not children for families"; agencies that don't, one observer notes, are more adoption "services" than agencies and tend to follow a predictable path. These organizations operate for a few years and offer little beyond basic child matching. Initially, several successful adoptions might be processed, and a comfortable profit will be made. Then, details start to be overlooked, including the continued reliability of intercountry contacts. Complaints mount up, financial pressures build, and the agency abruptly shuts its doors and cuts off contact with its caseload of prospective adoptive parents. Clients have no choice but to grit their teeth and move on, with partial—if any—refund of the fees they paid.

A troublesome aspect of intercountry adoption is that there have been few ways to keep track of fraudulent adoption schemes or individual operators other than by word of mouth or through informal contact between agencies. Recently, though, the International Alliance for Professional Accountability in Latin American Adoptions has attempted to do this. Their newsletter, *International Alliance Advocate*, publishes news and updates for adoption professionals on trends in intercountry adoption. The most disturbing items are warnings about schemes to defraud adoptive parents. These range from demands for large cash payments before the adoption process is underway to the deliberate concealment by foreign lawyers of a child's origin or health problems. In one recent alert, a writer warned against a lawyer operating in Peru. "Not one of the children originally assigned to any family was the child they ended up with," he reports. How much heartbreak must those families have experienced when they realized that the one key person they had trusted enough to make the long trip down to South America was actually taking advantage of them. And how much else might this lawyer have concealed from those families?

In such instances, the blame for fraudulent activity obviously rests on the shoulders of dishonest foreign contacts who deliberately take advantage of parents' emotional vulnerability and unfamiliarity with language, customs, and legal procedures. But in other cases, parents, too, share equal responsibility in cases of illegality. In their hurry to find a child to adopt with a minimum of legal hassle and cultural contact, some parents have deliberately looked the other way in situations that are clearly suspicious. When adoptive parents refuse to demand details about a child's origin and proof of voluntary relinquishment by birthparents or conspire to obtain a child under illegal circumstances, they are engaging in criminal activity that makes them as guilty as the foreign contact they pay to do the dirty work for them. And their actions clearly impact on others. If one parent can pay large amounts of money, why can't the next one? If an adopter will look the other way when a child's origins can't be explained, why can't the next adoptive family? "It is an enormous leap of faith for host countries to allow foreign adoption," says Susan Cox of Holt International Children's Services. Whenever adoptive parents choose an illegal route, the faith of those countries and of the children who are adopted is betrayed. Ultimately, too, parents betray themselves by forming their families through dishonest means. How must it feel for a child whose adoption story has elements of secrecy or dishonesty, and for those parents as they confront their child's questions in the years to come?

Because countries that permit independent international adoptions continue to struggle with allegations of illegality by all parties involved in the adoption process, the future of such adoptions is unclear. Some foreign governments have taken steps to completely eliminate private contracts between birthparents and adoptive parents, preferring instead to assign the adoption process to a few adoption agencies sanctioned to operate within the country. Romania took this step in 1991; Peru did the same in 1993. Providing agency oversight will hopefully eliminate most irregularities, and convince all countries to take a close look at just who is benefiting financially from international adoption.

Many sensational press accounts about the money paid and to be made in international adoptions create a confusing and infuriating picture of shady deals in foreign countries where naive Americans are at a clear disadvantage. The truth is simpler, though still unsettling for most people unfamiliar with the workings of Third-World economies. Most poor countries operate on a system of compensation involving middle-level government officials who expect a little extra for carrying out their jobs. "Bribery is relatively common but is generally disapproved of except in its mildest forms, such as speeding up bureaucratic processes (where it may be considered analogous to the use of tips in other cultures)," explains William Hutchinson in *Living in Colombia* (Intercultural Press, 1987). Many adopters are bewildered and angered by this system, which in the United States is illegal and clearly unethical. It's illegal in Russia or Brazil or the Philippines but, as Hutchinson explains, "people [in Colombia] comply with the law . . . in order to avoid punishment rather than because the law is a reflection of a higher morality or truth. They feel freer to exercise their own judgment with respect to laws." Though this helps explain a loosely condoned system of bribery, it sets no boundaries for adoptive parents who don't know how to draw the line between paying a tip or being extorted. For most people, it's an extremely uncomfortable judgment call that when viewed from the outside sounds less like local custom and more like illegal activity. Unfortunately, there are few guidelines. For some people, paying $10 to get a document processed is . . . well . . . acceptable. But what about $50? $100? What about $1,000?

When things are this confusing, wild assumptions and elaborated stories make all intercountry adoptions appear to be universally corrupt. The media hasn't helped. "Psst! Babies for Sale!" reads one particular juicy headline in a clipping from my files. Similar stories feed the idea that all intercountry adopters are suspect, all children adopted internationally must simply be products bought by foreigners whose own country ran out of stock. "How much did she cost?" asked a neighbor on meeting my daughter for the first time. Her question stunned and angered me. It was my first realization that to some she is seen as an exotic purchase rather than the daughter we had waited so long for. Even friends who know us well and know the story of Cristina's adoption still shake their heads at the complex process we went through. But, I think, what wouldn't they have gone through to bring their own children through a risky labor and delivery? That's the way I would describe Jean's, or my, or any adoptive parent's journey.

No adoption, especially an international one, is simple or easily explainable to an outside observer. The process involves hundreds of decisions and details; and like a trail of dominoes, when one piece crashes, all others follow. It's no wonder that Jean, after the failure of her adoption attempt, isn't sure if she can "face starting from scratch again, putting all of these documents together for another long and frustrating process." Intercountry adoption, with its added international complexities, makes the decision to start over even more difficult.

Does such struggle make us appreciate our children more, once we do become parents? I don't believe that any amount of pain can make our love better or more valid, or that we have to experience sorrow in order to know happiness. As Harold Kushner says in *When Bad Things Happen to Good People*, "All we can do is try to rise beyond the question 'Why did it happen?' and begin to ask the question 'What do I do now that it has happened?'"

"Somehow, This Feels Different . . . "

I felt awkward at our first meeting with each of our children. Both boys were handed over to us by the director of the orphanage, and we weren't given the opportunity to be alone with either child at the initial meeting. While in the director's presence, I felt I had to react like I was instantly bonding with the child, had to show how pleased I was ("Oh, look, isn't he so handsome?"). This lasted for about fifteen minutes and then we had to leave, since the next couple was waiting to meet their baby. We got back into the car and drove away from the orphanage. Especially with our first son, I remember feeling almost like I was kidnapping this little baby. Or that I was babysitting—I wondered if he was *really mine?* **(MD)**

O ur first child was escorted from Korea home to us. But the next time around, I asked if it was an option to go over there. I thought it might be cheaper to do it that way, for one thing; money was a big issue for us. I asked hesitantly; they said yes, but weren't real encouraging. So I did some legwork: I called around and discovered that it would cost just as much to fly to Seoul and stay in a hotel two nights as it would to have her escorted.

I wanted to go to Korea and be the one to pick her up at the orphanage. She was ten months old and had been institutionalized all that time. I just didn't want her to have any more intermediaries (an escort) in her life. I really felt that she needed to have me simplify her transition to us. I knew because of her special needs she hadn't been in a foster care situation, and the one person they told me she had formed an attachment to was a nun who only stopped in at the orphanage occasionally. So when I did come to take her home, the bonding was so powerful. She was a real loyal little person, I think because there had not yet been one person to bond with in all that time. Her first opportunity to really attach was with me.   **(FEM)**

My daughter flew from Moscow to LaGuardia Airport along with a group of five other children. She was escorted by her nurse from the orphanage. I spoke a very small amount of Russian; both she and her nurse spoke no English, so I couldn't ask anything.

Her first night home was a nightmare. Her disability, which I thought I knew all about, was far worse than they had told me; her limp was very bad. And she was out of control. She screamed, banged her head against the wall . . . it was pretty awful. Now, things are great. But that initial adjustment was one of the most difficult times of my life.   **(LM)**

I flew to Tegucigalpa, the capital of Honduras, for my daughter Grace's adoption. My adoption coordinator and the lawyer and a translator she had assembled met me at the airport. It was a Sunday, and the meeting was very festive, very celebratory. We loaded my luggage into a car and drove into the city.

Grace was abandoned at a state hospital. After she spent a month there, she was transferred to a state orphanage in Tegucigalpa. My adoption coordinator had found me a lawyer, Olga, who was wonderful in many respects, especially in her care of my daughter. Once my coordinator had assigned my case to her, Olga had brought milk and medicine to Grace at the orphanage. Milk was the main source of nourishment for the babies, but there was very little of it and it was diluted. Lots of children were sick, Grace included, with scabies, chronic ear infections, that sort of thing. Olga went every week to give Grace extra care.

The rules said I couldn't see the baby on a Sunday. But Olga happened to know somebody in charge, so we went over to the orphanage. I was terrified. I simply had no idea what to expect; I really was in an emotional daze. We were told at the orphanage that we couldn't go beyond the waiting area, so we sat for about ten minutes. Then all of a sudden, a door opened and a bassinet was rolled out and there ... was Grace!

I reacted all at once. "Oh. OH! Why, she looks like a normal baby." Then, "But she looks ... a little glazed over. Is she really OK?" I knew about the problem of institutionalized children who aren't held enough, haven't had enough stimulation. I was suddenly worried. What, it occurred to me, didn't I know about this baby? And then, after another split second, I stopped simply observing and my emotions broke through: "Oh, my God, this really is it! This is a child, a person, a human being, and she is my responsibility. This child is really mine, and I am her mother!"

I picked her up. Everybody oohed and aahed. Two staff workers explained that Gracie was a favorite of the nursery and obviously showed their affection for her. That reassured me about her care and about her. But at that point, so quickly after my first worried thoughts about her, my concerns were gone. I was too busy just being there with her, too busy just taking her in. I was allowed to spend a few minutes more, and then they took her from me and wheeled her away. No! I wanted to say. Why are you taking my baby? How amazing that my feelings solidified so fast. **(PR)**

Getting our son wasn't the highly charged emotional scene we thought it would be. It was very confusing, and much like being in shock. When we drove up to our hotel, our new son and an orphanage worker were waiting for us. Our coordinator ran out to our car and said, "Welcome! Your baby is right here." We were panicked; we didn't want to meet our child on the sidewalk. But out walked the attendant with this little bundle in her arms. She handed the baby to us ... and immediately, he started to cry. Quick, feed him! they all said. But our formula and bottles were packed away, there was no purified water like we had read you were supposed to mix formula with, and besides, I had NO prior experience in being an instant mom. It was kind of awful! **(FC)**

After I had met my son's birthmother and my son had been relinquished to me, I was driven to an apartment that had been reserved in my name. My luggage was unloaded for me and then everyone left. And there I was, in a strange apartment in a foreign city, alone with this newborn baby who was now my son. Fortunately, there was an adoptive couple living across the hall. They had been there a month and had a two-month-old boy. They were really happy to see me. And the landlady was really nice, so it was actually OK after that first night. The next day someone came to take me out to shop for groceries. And of course as soon as I got my son to bed that first night, I called my family to tell them that I had this beautiful new baby. But basically I was alone with this tremendous responsibility: I had to be feeding the baby, feeding myself, trying to learn all this new stuff ... I was in shock, and it seemed I had so much to do. There wasn't any special moment in which I bonded with him; I was too busy otherwise. I'm not certain ... but I think bonding took place over the course of the first week.   **(FS)**

Along with everything else we took to China, Jim and I packed along a video camera. An old, heavy one. We thought, We'll videotape that special moment of meeting our daughter for the first time.

We traveled in a group of adoptive parents. It took us practically three days of nonstop travel to get to Changsha, China. Once there, each family had to be interviewed by this team of Chinese officials, two young women, in our hotel. Of course, they addressed all questions to the man, which I'm not used to. But finally, at the end of our interview, one of the women looked at me and said, "I know your daughter." Jim stopped talking. We stared at the woman. She explained that she liked to visit the orphanage and play with the children "because they're so pure," and that she loved seeing our daughter.

Both of us were low-level shaking. We had just arrived after three days of travel and all, but this kind of trembling wasn't from being tired. "I have a picture of her," the woman said to me. I felt tears coming. They handed us Mimi's little passport photo that had been taken only a couple of weeks before. I was prepared for ... well ... not the cutest baby—just to keep things in perspective. But that picture was of the cutest baby I had ever seen in my life! "Don't tell the others," said the women. "They didn't get pictures."

After that experience it was very difficult to focus. By two o'clock that afternoon, we could hardly stand it. Finally, along with our adoption group, we drove by van five miles in 100- degree weather to the Changsha orphanage. At the door to the building, Jim turned on the video camera. We walked through a series of dim rooms until we reached one that was cooler than the others. Probably thirty babies lay in low bamboo cribs with a few nurses in attendance. We were trying to hold on to each other. A nurse leaned over, picked up a baby, held her up in the air and said "Li Mi!!"—our baby's name! And Mimi, as we now call her, burst into this beautiful smile. I knew she was smiling directly at me. I knew it! (What I didn't know at the time was that she loves being up in the air too).

So there's our special moment of seeing Mimi for the first time, and we were overwhelmed and overjoyed . . . and the video came out all ceilings and floors! **(RC)**

Jean's Journal

June 7, 1990

It is a slow June afternoon at the end of the academic year. I have had too much lunch, and am utterly unable to do any serious work. My wandering eyes catch the phone number taped to my lamp. What the hell . . .

A pleasant woman answers the phone. She says her name is Shirley. Yes, she says, she will be happy to send me information about the relief agency's work. She says they are arranging adoptions in Mexico, Honduras, and Peru. I tell her a little about myself and my adoption experience, and give her Julie's name when she asks how I got this phone number. Shirley tells me a little about the agency's work, and about the profound poverty they encounter in Central and South America. While many agencies believe it is better to help children without removing them from their families and their cultures, the steadily worsening economic situation has led this one to conclude reluctantly that the only way to save some of these children immediately is to place them for adoption. As I hang up, I am struck by how different this conversation was from the ones I used to have with John and Margaret.

For a half hour or so, I read a professional journal and wonder if there is any graceful way to leave the office this early. At two o'clock my phone rings. The receptionist tells me Shirley is on the line. I think probably she has lost my address.

Shirley's voice is strong and clear. She has just finished a long phone conversation with Julie. One of the agency's contacts was approached last night by a mother who wishes to surrender her two-day-old baby girl for adoption. The agency's policy is not to take custody of a child until they have a potential placement, and no one on their waiting list is willing to go where this child is. If I were willing to go to the Amazon jungle, and she would certainly understand if a single woman were not, the child could be mine. I could leave as soon as my papers are recompiled and sent to Peru. When I say I am interested, Shirley says she will send a packet of materials to me express this afternoon. She says God has sent me to them.

It doesn't happen like this, I tell myself as I hang up the phone. After two years I should know that by now. But somehow, this feels different. Long dormant emotions stir beneath my numbness. I must tell someone. I walk down the hall toward Phyllis's office, Phyllis who has waited with me since the beginning. I haven't talked much about adoption with her or anyone in a long time, and I wonder what I will say. "Could you cover a few summer school classes for me if I'm called out of town?" I begin.

A broad smile breaks across her face. "It's Jessie, isn't it? You have your baby."

June 8

Just as Shirley had promised, papers from her agency have arrived overnight. I called her immediately with a list of the questions hard experience has taught me to ask:

What is known about the child? Is she healthy? Has anyone from the agency seen her? What is her current legal status? What are the laws in Peru if the mother wishes to change her mind? This child, Shirley said, seems small but otherwise quite healthy. Her mother is a mature woman who has other children to support. The child has been surrendered to a foster mother in Iquitos, Peru. Formal surrender, however, does not occur in Peru until the adoptive parent(s) arrive to take custody of the baby. The physical surrender will be carefully documented with photographs and witnesses, so there can be no question later of coercion. The legal surrender happens subsequently at the courthouse, where the adoption will later be finalized.

How smoothly are adoptions proceeding these days in Peru? How long are parents having to stay there? I am worried about the stories of other parents who ended up in Peru for many, many weeks. Shirley assured me that things move more quickly in out-of-the-way places, although Iquitos is a brand-new site and therefore an unknown in terms of time. Their contacts there are optimistic about time—two to three weeks, they are saying now.

What will this *really* cost? What fees does this rather substantial check I'm supposed to send the agency cover? Shirley explained that a portion of the check covers the agency's expenses. The remainder goes to the Peruvian woman, Charo, who works as an independent "adoption consultant" to international adoption programs and whose contacts led to this child. She, in turn, hires a Peruvian lawyer and pays all but some minor court costs and the costs of the visa and passport the child must have to leave the country. The mother receives only moneys to cover her expenses during pregnancy and delivery. Charo is adamant that what she does hasn't the slightest appearance of baby selling about it.

Can I talk to other parents who have worked with this agency? Can I talk to Charo myself? Shirley willingly gave me Charo's phone number. Charo has seen the baby and arranged for a lawyer; she will return to the States in about a week and a half. Charo can give me the names of many families with whom she has worked.

Finally, how quickly can this agency process my completed application? If this is "the right Jessie," she is already growing up without me. Shirley said it will probably take them several weeks after receiving my paperwork to have it certified, authorized, signed, and sealed in a dozen state and federal offices and in the Peruvian consulate; then it will be sent to Peru for translation. I asked if there were a way to speed this up. She told me that because I live in Chicago and could physically go to these government offices, it would almost surely be faster for me to assemble the dossier according to Peruvian requirements. After what happened in my first agency, I think I would feel better to do this for myself, though if I do, I can't exactly figure out what my agency fee pays for—except for Charo's name and phone number. And if this child is my daughter, it's probably worth it.

June 12

I have spent the last two days running around Chicago like a crazy person, trying to create my Peruvian adoption dossier. When I stop to take an internal inventory tonight, I am surprised to discover that I am a little angry. Then I realize that I more than vaguely suspect this may be yet another wild goose chase, and an incredible waste of my time, energy, and spirit. I keep waiting for the phone to ring with the sad news that the referral has fallen through. But I also know that there will never, ever be another chance if I don't follow through on this one.

Slowly, very slowly, I am telling people what is going on. My banker, who had to cut the check for the adoption agency. Lonnie and Naomi, who are cautiously pleased. My dean, who once again tries to figure out a leave of absence for me. And my sister. She has worked her way through whatever doubts she had at the beginning about my adopting, and is clearly excited when she hears I have once again ordered plane tickets for South America. Then, I tell her my destination is not Paraguay but the Amazon jungle.

Over the phone, I hear my mother's voice: "Isn't that . . . interesting."

June 18

The saga continues . . .

Tonight, I had two phone calls. The first was from Charo. I liked everything about her on the phone: her openness, her willingness to admit what she did and did not really know, her integrity. She says she wants to meet me before I go to Peru. Because she will not be there, I will be on my own for a while in the jungle, and she says she wants to be sure that I will know how to manage by myself. She says she needs to be able to say honestly to Peruvian authorities that she has met me, interviewed me. She is having a picnic in St. Louis on Sunday, June 24, to which all her adoptive parents have been invited. It will be a chance for me to hear many stories, to see many children, to get helpful hints on what to take and what to expect when I get to South America. I am scheduled to leave on Tuesday, the 26th, for Lima. It seems impossible to make this picnic trip too, and yet I know I must.

The other phone call was from a man who is just back after many weeks in Peru; his wife is still in Lima, completing the adoption of a baby girl. He was given my name by a friend who thought it would be helpful for me to speak to someone with recent experience. My caller told me horror stories of bribery, dishonesty, filth, and crime. Everyone is "on the take," he said. He told me not to let my child out of my sight; he said that I could not be sure I would get the same child back.

Dear God! What have I gotten myself into?

June 20

Panic has seized me by the throat. I know I must make this trip if the child continues to be available to me. But, to what kind of a place am I going?

Yesterday and today, I tried to do things to reassure myself, to protect myself and this possible child however I can. Dear Monsignor E has written to the Vincentian community in Lima; he has also called a community of sisters there, who will give me a place to stay if I need one. The banker has written letters of reference to Peruvian banks, in case I run out of money. My contact in the senator's office, who has patiently worked with me on visa problems throughout this long process, has managed a letter of introduction from the senator. God only knows where I might need that. My doctor has given me prescriptions for everything from intestinal problems to dengue fever.

I have visited several pediatricians and selected one who has agreed to see the baby immediately on our return, if and when that may be. He recommends that I take to Peru a soy-based baby formula (many children have a lactose intolerance); he thinks two cases (two actual cases?) of the powder should probably be enough. The doctor also suggests that I bring baby Tylenol drops and some Pedialyte, which I gather is used to prevent dehydration in children who have intestinal problems. In addition to packing clothes for myself and this child for two climates (it's always summer in the Amazon, but it's winter now in Lima) for an indeterminate period of time, I've bought a case (more than 250!) of disposable diapers. Charo has recommended that I bring gifts for the biological mother, my lawyer, and the judge. And people tell me to bring a stroller from here. I am used to traveling light. I think I will look like I'm moving to Peru.

All of this, for a child I still suspect I may never see.

June 24

Today, I went to a picnic in St. Louis. I am glad to have met Charo and to know that a *real* person has found this child for me, instead of merely the voices on the phone from Michigan. I am glad to have met so many adoptive parents at the picnic. They rave about Charo, about her integrity and her care. One new father called her a "Peruvian Mother Theresa."

But what was best of all was to see these new families safely home with their beautiful children, all colors and shapes and sizes of children and yet all Peruvian. Yes, these families have their stories to tell, and many had problems while in South America. But the difficult parts of their stories are fading now, diminished by the delight they obviously feel in their new little ones.

I think this must be like a difficult pregnancy: however terrible the experience, when it ends with a healthy, happy child, you forget what came before it.

June 25

Tomorrow, God willing, I leave for Peru. Even if they call me in the morning to tell me the adoption has fallen through, I will probably go to South America anyway and try to locate another child myself.

Tonight, I must try to sleep if I am to be able to manage these next few days. Of course, I can never sleep when I must. I have made many, many lists, and they roll on and on in my head like some bad jingle from a television commercial: what I should take to Iquitos, what I should pack but leave here to be sent later if needed, what I should tell the house sitter, what phone numbers I should have, and what phone numbers those people should have so they can call others . . .

Suddenly, I realize I can't remember where I've packed certain essential things. In particular, I can't remember where I've put my new Swiss Army knife with the corkscrew. I blame this particular form of madness on Peggy, who says she can travel anywhere in the world with dry matches and a Swiss Army knife. Phyllis, who has helped with the last of the packing and is sleeping in the guestroom tonight, hears me on the staircase. As I am pulling on my jeans over my nightgown, I tell her that I am going out to the garbage cans to look for my Swiss Army knife, which I somehow threw away when I cleaned out the refrigerator. I also tell her that I realize I may finally have lost my mind. With a look of patient tolerance, she settles herself at the kitchen table while I make my way to the alley. It is two o'clock in the morning.

I will remember many things about these last few weeks in the days and years to come. But I suspect that what I will remember most clearly about tonight is standing barefoot in the alley, searching unsuccessfully beneath the three-bean salad for a Swiss Army knife with a corkscrew.

June 26

Dearest Jessie,

As I sit on a plane bound for Lima, Peru, I finally dare to write to you again. My head still knows that many things can go wrong, but my soul is somehow certain that, at long last, I am going to pick up my daughter.

I can hardly believe my good fortune. Not only am I going to adopt a little girl barely a month old, but I am going to a country I have always wanted to see, and to the Amazon rain forest, which I first studied in grade school. There will be so much to teach you about the proud history of Peru and its people, and about that beautiful and varied country that includes tropical jungles, rugged mountains, and one of the world's two fog deserts where Lima is built. I have arranged to stay in Lima for a day or two, both to launch the necessary paperwork at the American embassy and to have a bit of time to learn something about the city; I imagine as we come back on our way home, I will be more interested in getting you safely back to the States than in sight-seeing.

Wong and Phyllis drove me to the airport this morning. I did not acquit myself well there: I took them to the wrong airline terminal, and kept talking all morning about going to Paraguay. We all cried when I finally got on the plane. Now I keep remembering the Spanish lesson of long ago in which I learned how to say that my luggage has been lost and has gone to Amsterdam. No doubt Wong and Phyllis are even now wondering if my luggage is the only thing headed in the wrong direction.

June 28

Dear Jessie,

My second grey day in Lima. For six months of the year, the fog rolls in off the Pacific across the warmer desert land on which Lima is built, and then is trapped by the Andes mountains, which tower like a wall behind the city. The humidity penetrates everything; my clothes feel damp when I take them out of the suitcase. I am grateful that whatever I find in the Amazon, at least there will be sunshine.

Charo's sister, Vicky, along with my lawyer, Dr. A, and his associate, all met me at the chaotic Lima airport late on June 26. Then, somehow, the four of us and all my luggage and my case of diapers struggled into Vicky's Volkswagen beetle for the drive into town. I was not optimistic about my Spanish after this drive; everyone was excited and talked incredibly fast with an accent totally unfamiliar to my ear. Whenever anyone addressed me and smiled expectantly in my direction, I nodded and answered, "Si." So far as I know, this strategy worked fairly well and I haven't yet agreed to anything I may regret later. At least I could read the papers Dr. A gave me to sign when we arrived at the *hostal*; he left yesterday for Iquitos to get the adoption process started before I arrive.

There are many Americans in this *hostal* on the outskirts of Lima, and they form a sort of expatriate community of adoptive families. One family here has a baby son who is the ninth child of his biological family. During his mother's pregnancy, his father was killed by terrorists in the highlands, leaving an illiterate nineteen-year-old boy the head of the family. Like so many others, the family came to Lima in search of safety and work; so far, they have found little of either. Another family is adopting the child of impoverished parents. Because Peruvian law makes it very difficult for married parents to surrender for adoption a child born legitimately, the mother has said on the official papers that this baby is the child of a stranger who seduced her in a taxicab. Similar stories are told all the time by families too poor to support their children and too responsible to throw them away. A third couple is adopting two children simultaneously, a boy and a girl, both under the age of three months. They say it will be easier than coming back again in a year or two. A fourth family is adopting a beautiful three-year-old boy, Luis, who was left at an orphanage shortly after his birth. He has lived in that orphanage all his life until a few weeks ago when his American parents brought him to this *hostal*. Luis can be all sweetness and light one moment, then suddenly grab something and run into another room like a thief; no doubt these are the skills of survival that have helped him reach the age of three. There is also one single adoptive mother here, Joan, whose daughter was born in Iquitos though she was surrendered for adoption here. I try to absorb Joan's quiet strength for the days ahead.

While everyone seems delighted with their beautiful Peruvian children (and, for all their variety, they do all seem to me beautiful with their dark eyes and thick black hair), with a few notable exceptions these families also seem frustrated and burned out. Although they have all been here several weeks at least, many have seen relatively little of Lima or even of the area of Miraflores in which the *hostal* is located; when I ask about the famous Nasca lines just outside of Lima, no one has visited them. The women seem to prefer to stay in the *hostal* with their children while the men go exploring, as if they, as mothers, will never one day have to answer their children's questions about the land where they were born. Only a handful of these parents have learned even a few words of Spanish; few have tried the local Peruvian restaurants, preferring instead the Chinese takeout of the neighborhood *chifa*. Perhaps what I am seeing in them is the outcome of the long and frustrating legal process that for the most part still lies before me. Perhaps it is in part the result of the sleepless nights of new parents, followed by endless days without sunlight made still longer by regular power failures and water outages; one woman here has had shampoo in her hair for several days. Many of these parents have also been sick, with colds and flu and intestinal disorders; in less than forty-eight hours, I already feel the beginnings of a chest cold as the pollution and fog penetrate. Perhaps this is also the product of a profound sense of isolation from home and family, from things familiar, from a language they understand. For whatever reasons, many of these Americans talk about the Peruvians as "those people," not seeming to realize quite yet that their new son or daughter is also one of "those people." My heart breaks for them all as they count the weary days and weeks till they can finally go home.

It is easy for me, still fresh from the States and buoyant in the expectation of meeting my baby, to be judgmental. But I know that I will have it easier than nearly everyone I have met here. I have traveled in the Third World before, and have some idea of what to expect, what precautions to take. I have some simple command of the language around me, at least if people talk slowly enough, and I can read the papers they ask me to sign. I am going somewhere warm and sunny, to a place I have always wanted to visit and with enough money to afford a few excursions to see the sites. I have left no partner or other children behind in the States to long for as the days crawl by; I think, in fact, that wherever you and I can be together is where I'll want to be.

I hope that I can spend whatever time I have in Peru learning as much as I can about this incredibly rich culture and its people, and practicing the language. Already I imagine coming back here when you are older, perhaps to take a visiting appointment at a university, so that we can really know what it means to live in Peru. I hope that I can learn enough in these few weeks to help you feel proud of the land where you were born, and to help other families who come here enjoy this experience with their own children. I remember Charo's picnic last weekend and the people there who helped me prepare for this trip with infinite gratitude.

Today my father, son of the first Jessie Knoll, would have been eighty-three years old. Tomorrow, God willing, I will meet his granddaughter.

June 29

Dear Jessie,

I have learned that regardless of schedule, Aero Peru flights leave when everyone gets there. And so I waited, stranded for seven long hours in the Lima airport. Now, at last, I am flying over the Andes toward Iquitos. It was grey and foggy in the city, but here, high above the mountains and clouds, the sun is setting in pinks and purples.

I had expected to feel nervous and afraid these last few hours. Instead, it seems more like the night before Christmas, when there is magic in the air. I owe much of this to my lawyer's associate, Dr. G, who sat with me all those hours in the airport, making reassuring conversation with the help of my Spanish-English dictionary. He laughed when I told him that I had *mariposas en el estómago* (butterflies in my stomach), and he fed me flat Coke and dry toast in the airport *cantina*. I tried to forget that because I am carrying more cash than I will probably need, Dr. G was visibly wearing a gun.

Sunset does not last long near the equator, and it is suddenly quite dark. I have no idea how long this flight is, but I feel the plane going down. There are no city lights below, only the reflection of the moon on a twisting, turning body of water I assume is some part of the Amazon River. I cannot tell where we are in relation to the ground until suddenly, with a thump, we have landed. Is it possible we have arrived?

I walk slowly down the airsteps and toward the simple building that is the terminal. I realize I could be anywhere in the world (who knows where Aero Peru might take me?) until I see Dr. A's broad smile. It seems like hundreds of little boys rush across the runway to carry baggage from the plane. A handsome young man who turns out to be Alex, my translator and the manager of the *hostal* where I will stay, marshals a few of them into a group and organizes my multiple pieces of baggage into several *motocarros*, little three-wheeled conveyances that remind me of the motorized rickshaws (appropriately called *tuk tuks)* in Southeast Asia. Whatever may have happened to my suitcases, I am grateful to see that the case of diapers has made it all the way to the jungle.

As we putter along the poorly paved road lined with thatched houses, Dr. A tells me that the mother and my baby have been waiting all day at the *hostal*. He asks if I want to meet my baby in the lobby or in my room. I suppose I had the quaint notion that I would have time to wash my face and comb my hair before I became a mother, but this seems unlikely now. When I say I'd prefer to meet you in my room, Alex tells me not to stop at the desk to check in.

I am standing amidst the chaos of boys and young men delivering my luggage when suddenly the room grows very still. Someone says softly, "La bebita." I turn and see first your foster mother, Rosalita, and then your mother, Maria, standing in the doorway holding a tiny bundle. In Lima, parents told me to expect you to be dirty and poorly clothed; instead, you are dressed in a pink nylon dress and lace socks, smelling of baby powder and sleeping peacefully in Maria's arms. Maria is tiny and delicate, with skin the color of yours. She smiles sweetly as she places you in my arms, and tells me she calls you Topacio, her little topaz. We are both crying as Dr. A takes our picture. I stumble through some Spanish, which I intend will tell her that you are a miracle to me, and that I will love and care for you always, but I realize even my English is inadequate for this extraordinary moment. Quite soon, Maria is gone.

There are two other American families here in the *hostal*, and they, too, have been waiting all day for my arrival. Debbie and Terry have adopted a son, Joey, now about eight weeks old; Katie, whose husband and son have already gone home, has adopted Cristina, an eleven-month-old who crawls happily among my locked suitcases. In a few minutes you stir and wake and begin to insist, so gently, on your right to be fed. But in the confusion, I haven't the slightest idea where the bottles or cans of formula can be, and I am frankly too preoccupied with holding you to be able to unpack. So I give each person a luggage key and ask them to open whatever they can with it, and to rustle around among the contents of my suitcases till we find what you need. In a short time, my clothes are scattered everywhere, and you are sucking enthusiastically on a bottle of soy formula.

I talk for a long time with these new friends and learn that they are all due to depart within a day or so. Still, tonight this tiny community of American adoptive parents thousands of miles from home has embraced us in the gentle and friendly way of the Peruvian people themselves. When they finally leave, Katie says, "Good night, Mom." As the door closes behind her, I am momentarily terrified in the way that all new mothers must be when their relatives finally go home.

It is nearly three o'clock in the morning now, and everything is perfectly still. I have told myself I am not going to be one of those neurotic mothers who wakes with a start every few minutes, fearful that something terrible has happened to her baby. No, not me.

Instead, it seems I will simply not go to sleep at all, preferring instead to watch you as you sleep on the bed beside me, stroking your hair and counting your toes again and again. I wonder if you sense the activity that brought you here, or recognize that inexperienced hands feed and change you now. I promised Maria that I would love and care for her little jewel all my life. Please be patient, dear, beautiful Jessie, as I learn how.

By the way: Happy birthday, Papa.

"Somehow, This Feels Different . . . "

commentary

I sit here for a moment after reading Jean's words and find it hard to write much just yet. I'm supposed to use this section to discuss the experience of temporary life in a foreign country, but I'm too caught in my own memories. It hasn't been long since we left Peru with our daughter in the summer of 1990, but I know that the country's problems have intensified. The political scene is even more turbulent. Just getting by is more difficult now than ever for most Peruvians. The intercountry adoption process is going through revision, but there's no certainty that the new law will make the process any faster. And living in Peru while completing an adoption can be exhausting and demoralizing, as the country's difficult economic situation affects both citizens and foreigners alike.

But for those who adopt internationally, the hardships and exhilarations of life inside a troubled country take a backseat to the overwhelming emotions you experience on first meeting the child you've waited so long for. That particular memory will be etched on my brain forever, long after the ink has faded on our stack of documents and the adoption papers are filed away. I remember the small details: that Cristina felt surprisingly heavy and slightly soggy, every inch a nine-month-old. Her birthmother had carefully dressed her and slipped her little feet into shiny black shoes, for (as I was to find out later) only the very poorest wear no shoes. As I took her into my arms for the first time, I smelled a strange, funny kind of sweetness; no wonder, her bottle was filled with a standard formula of half evaporated milk, half water, and two teaspoons of sugar.

But oh, Cristina, your birthmama . . . how beautiful she was. I couldn't take my eyes off her, because someday, I thought, you will look so much like her. As she cried inconsolably, I cried, too, for all of us and for all that had brought us to this moment. "It is traditional," said my adoption coordinator softly in my ear, "to kiss your child's mother and offer her your thanks." How awkward I felt, how completely inadequate, how grateful and how very sad. And, despite all I wanted to tell her, how frustrating it was to have little more than a kiss and "muchas gracias" to offer.

That moment was for me the epitome of culture shock. If I had felt over my head up to that point after arriving late at night in a foreign city where armed soldiers patrolled street corners, I now felt really lost as I struggled to take it all in—strange surroundings, little sleep, unfamiliar faces, a weeping young mother, and a new baby, wide eyed and quiet, clearly wondering at the strange words coming out of my mouth. My ability to communicate, at the time I needed it the most, was gone.

Culture shock is defined as a reaction, in several stages, to the loss of leaving a familiar environment, and disorientation at entering the new. Adoptive parents barely have time to experience the initial excitement of a new culture—stage one of culture shock—before they receive their children and plunge into all the responsibilities of parenthood.

Stage two of culture shock is complicated and intensified by the unique situation most adopters find themselves in. When cultural differences begin to cause problems in day-to-day life, visitors to a foreign country tend to respond either by withdrawing, turning hostile, or on the other extreme, denying their own culture in favor of the new. I saw most of those reactions in myself and in other adoptive families I met. There were, for example, the parents who spent all their time caring for their children, barely leaving their rooms except to use the telephone or eat (though it's only fair to say that life with a new baby usually requires lots of attention and sleepless nights). I also remember watching a mother so angry at the hotel's faulty telephone system that she slammed the receiver down in front of a long-suffering desk clerk and stomped off in a rage. Few families, except those who are adopting for a second time, come well traveled and fully prepared, taking a new baby in stride, speaking fluent Spanish, and reveling in cultural differences, confident in the adoption process. The majority of adopters find themselves in a frustrating position: unprepared for the irregularities of daily life, ill with diarrhea, unable to communicate except through a translator, unfamiliar with a strange environment, and overwhelmed by parenthood.

It's not always as bad as all that. But what does create a constant level of stress for all adopters is the status of their adoption case as it makes its way through a country's court system. Even if your lawyer gives you every assurance that the matter is completely out of your hands, the greatest cause for worry is that it is completely out of your hands. And that's a new feeling, after making so many preparations at home for the adoption.

Two months before we traveled to South America, Peter and I spent countless hours putting together our dossier for Peru. Most parents planning an international adoption have to do it. You painstakingly assemble all the official papers required for adoption in that particular country—birth certificates, marriage certificates and divorce decrees (if applicable), police clearances, fingerprint cards, several different letters of recommendation, doctors' reports, a psychological report, the homestudy (each country has different requirements, but this is more or less the list). Each document must then be notarized locally, certified by your state, and authenticated by the foreign country's U.S. embassy. In addition, you must remember to have the FBI clear your fingerprints and file your INS paperwork (I-600A, Application for Advance Processing of Orphan Petition), which will eventually enable you to get a U.S. visa for your child before she enters her new country. Yes, it's a headache. But you have the list, you do it and get it done, and you're in control. And if you're like us, you can't imagine you'll ever have to worry about any more paperwork, considering the wad you end up accumulating.

When I think back on it, I realize our dossier work first gave me an idea of the effect this kind of bureaucracy would have on me. I felt proud when we finished the dossier, but I was angry too. Why should we have to go through this? Wasn't our homestudy enough? Why should the Peruvian government need to know about our infertility treatment? Why did we have to pay the embassy $32 to authenticate each of our documents? Without knowing it at the time, I was already exhibiting culture shock with my anger over Cultural Differences That Cause Problems. Yet I had no idea of the bureaucracy yet to come!

As difficult as life may be after arriving in your child's birth country, though, lashing out with criticism and anger is probably the worst reaction to this phase of both culture shock and the adoption process. If families can remain patient during this often difficult time of personal tensions, homesickness, depression, or withdrawal, they have a better chance of forging an important bond to their child's birth country, something that will come to be invaluable as their child grows.

Happily, many adoptive parents move quickly into Culture Shock, stage three. Reaching this phase means settling in, adjusting to a foreign lifestyle, even developing pride in being able to cope with difficulties and helping out those who have newly arrived. There is also pleasure in being able to use the language just a little. I remember practicing over and over "Cristina es mi hija adoptada" (Cristina is my daughter by adoption), and feeling grandly competent when people's confusion changed to smiles of understanding. Again, the standard adjustment most people experience in stage three is complicated for adopters because of continued anxiety over the adoption process. It's hard to relax and enjoy the pleasures of an interesting new culture while you're worrying. At this point, your paperwork has probably begun its journey through the courts, and it's often a couple of days between each progress report from your lawyer or coordinator. The aggravation of not hearing much about those precious documents and the impatience over delays can keep most adopters from sleeping. Are there problems with my documents? Is my child's birthmother having second thoughts? Did the embassy get my paperwork from the INS? Managing anxiety is easier when making a conscious effort to see and experience as much of a new culture as possible.

This can be a challenge. First, you may be spending hours waiting in lines, keeping appointments to get documents signed, or attending to details that eat up all your time and energy. Even if you have a lawyer to do most of these things for you, inevitably you'll still have to do a good amount of footwork. Second, even if you have too much time on your hands and know you have to keep yourself busy, you may not be anxious to leave the comfort or safety of the house or hotel in which you're staying. But after a while, there's just so much you have to do to attend to your new child's needs, and just so much boredom you can stand. And it helps to keep in mind the long-term benefits of adopting your child in her own birth country: as witness to her origins, you will be able to bring back a wealth of priceless, positive memories to relive as your child grows.

Two weeks after we arrived in Peru, my husband and son returned to the United States, leaving me and our new daughter to complete the adoption, however long that might take. I vividly remember standing in the middle of the road with Cristina in my arms, tears streaming down my face, waving at the disappearing *motocarro* as it took Peter and Matt away to the airport. How will I survive now? I remember thinking. We had leaned on each other heavily for the first difficult two weeks of adjustment; now, just as we were beginning to settle in somewhat, most of my family was gone and there I was, on my own with my new daughter, feeling scared and utterly alone. I struggled with the urge to run up to my room, lock myself in, and cry for the rest of the day. Then I looked at Cristina. As she stared up at me, her little face seemed to ask, "Would somebody please tell me again what's happening to me?" It was the same expression I saw on the day her birthmother put her in my arms. We both feel lost, don't we? I thought. But you're depending on me. I'm in charge . . . I guess.

My fright at being on my own came mainly from the undeniable fact that although I had seen and done lots of fascinating things together with my family during the past two weeks, I tended to let Peter take the lead in most new experiences. I'm a braver person in the company of others, especially my mate. Being left on my own was hard, but ultimately did give me the incentive I needed to truly get to know Cristina's birth country. In fact, Peru eventually began to feel a little like my own backyard; and though in the end I was relieved to finally return home, I left behind a place that for six weeks had been a wonderful home, and friends I would especially miss in my first few months back in the United States. Maybe I had actually experienced a little of stage four of culture shock, when

adjustment becomes complete, when life in a foreign country becomes simply another way of being, no different or worse than the
one you knew in your native land. For me and for Cristina, I felt
blessed that through the Peruvian and American friends I made, I
was able to have even a little taste of feeling at home and at ease in
a country so different from my own.

I've come to believe that despite where you might go to adopt
and how hard it might be, the key to taking good feelings away
with you is getting to know even a couple of people you can call
friends, whom you can look back to with great fondness and
remember as a special link to the country that will forever be your
child's first homeland. At first, this seemed difficult to me. How to
communicate with no common language? How to find time, when
I was busy taking care of Cristina? How to find the courage, when
I felt so out of place and unsure of myself? Gradually, I saw that
opportunities often presented themselves. All of the clerks in the
hotel were studying English, and before leaving, Peter had swapped
English and Spanish lessons with one of them. Now Miguel asked
if I would do the same, and we had a hilarious time mispronounc-
ing words and trading dictionaries. Rosario, who also worked in
the hotel, told her English teacher one day about us. One evening
the whole class made an impromptu field trip to the hotel. What
excitement! Debbie and Terry and their new son Joey and Cristina
and I spent the next hour with ten eager new friends who visited us
often after that. They invited us to an English-speaking party. We
ate ice cream together at the town square. Some of us took a picnic
trip up the Napa River. I felt so grateful for their friendship and
interest in me. Each casual encounter with these new friends was a
great adventure for me, but the very greatest came one Saturday
evening. That night, Cristina and I were honored to be invited to
the wedding of our new friend Walter at a small church in the
Punchana district of Iquitos. It was a beautiful occasion I will never
forget, and a particularly significant one for me, as I realized that
Walter felt comfortable enough in our friendship to have me present at the most important occasion of his life. I felt grateful and
very excited.

Walter and Diana's wedding gave me the opportunity to more
closely observe how people interact in Latin American society. I
noticed at first the formality with which Walter greeted his guests
and introduced me to many of them. I followed the lead of two

friends who came with me and shook each person's hand. "¡Mucho gusto!" (Pleased to meet you!) everyone was saying. Several people smiled and held their arms out for Cristina. In fact, she spent the evening being passed happily from one admirer to the other. Children are accepted at practically any occasion, and the children themselves seem to understand that with this acceptance comes a responsibility: many little ones sat quietly and never lost patience, though at times they talked and giggled quietly. Despite the hubbub, most people, especially women, spoke very softly. I often found myself leaning forward to catch the words of a new acquaintance.

It took a while to get past introductions. It was important that everyone be introduced to everyone else, and that friends acknowledge each other properly before the ceremony began. Getting started on time seemed to make little difference; in general, this is usually true and is a real problem for many *norteamericanos* (as Americans are called). It's not that Latin Americans are indifferent to time passing, but that time is less important than peoples' needs and consideration of each other. Getting angry about this relaxed sense of time is rude, and has the appearance of challenging another person's importance or position—and is, therefore, counterproductive to any kind of personal or business transaction. We Americans can explode so quickly. Sometimes I wondered if Peruvians ever got angry, since on only one rare occasion did I ever hear voices raised. Later, I found out that anger is usually expressed in Latin America indirectly, such as in responding slowly (or not responding at all) to a request or demand.

The wedding ceremony was simple, but full of great dignity. Bridesmaids and groomsmen were dressed elaborately in outfits that Walter told me were all sewn by his new mother-in-law and her friends; a lot of work, yes, but not too unusual, since many Peruvians sew their own clothes. This explained something I had always puzzled at: despite the wide variety of beautiful dresses I saw women wearing on my daily stroll through town, the stores I visited never stocked such fine clothes. Later on, a friend brought me to a fabric shop where I found a dazzling variety of silks, rayon, and cotton, raw materials for the brilliant outfits I had admired so often. Women rarely wore shorts or pants, indicative of a greater sexual division than we experience in the United States, perhaps, and of a more traditional role many women still play in Latin

America. As Walter signed the official wedding registry book followed by Diana, I wondered if the traditional role of a married woman would limit her. Such a thought struck me as immediately absurd. For as I looked around me at the tin-roofed, concrete-brick church and remembered the poor neighborhood we had come through to get to the wedding, I knew that Diana and Walter's greatest limitations would be economic; for in their world, basic necessities are often luxuries.

After the wedding, we all crowded into the reception area, a tiny side room open to the air on one side. As the rain beat down, we feasted on delicious plates of beans, yuca (similar to mashed potatoes), and chicken. It would have been rude to refuse the huge amount of food set aside especially for me, and though I couldn't finish it, I ate a little of everything. Everyone applauded the speeches of welcome and thanks by the groom and bride. Gifts were proudly displayed, baskets of household articles elaborately packaged in clear yellow plastic that would be unwrapped privately by the newlyweds. Both gift giver and recipient would be equally embarrassed if presents were opened immediately and in public, since it would mean that the item was really needed, and the giver would therefore be participating in an act of charity.

What should my present be? I had asked anxiously before the wedding. Perhaps some photographs, I was told. Pictures of the bride and groom from your camera. Therefore I became the official wedding photographer, posing the bride and groom next to their beautiful cake and assembling the wedding party for a group shot.

Back in the United States a month later, I had the film developed and eagerly took a look at the pictures. All the combined festivity, strangeness, and seriousness of the occasion came back to me. Walter and Diana were members of a Baptist congregation, and the friends who had come to the wedding with me were disappointed by the lack of dancing and music. But the pictures held plenty of celebration and music for me! They were proof that I had been able to put aside my fumbling Spanish and awkwardness and feel at ease outside my own language and culture. In a funny way I felt I had crossed an invisible line, and felt enormously lucky at the opportunity.

After the wedding, some of us found a tiny cantina with a portable radio and several bottles of beer. Then we danced, and once again I felt honored in knowing that I was included not as the *gringa* who might otherwise have been lonely in her hotel room with a baby to take care of, but as a friend who laughed along with everyone else while Tia Norma showed us how to really dance the lambada.

How dreary my memories would be without the people I met during my stay in Peru. It's a little like flipping through a photo album. Shots of buildings and landscape are interesting, but limited; it's hard to imagine the opposite side of the street, or what the far shore of the river might look like. Once people start to populate the scenes, things begin to look much more interesting. Just who is this guy, and how did you get to know him? Who is she? Where did you meet her? All of a sudden the edges of the photograph expand, and the scene comes to life. The people have friends, who have other friends, who have brothers or aunts or wives or grandparents who want to meet you, or take you to a festival, or escort you to a wedding, or ask you about America, or help you buy oranges. You're back with them, remembering all the good times and conveniently forgetting the document delays, the homesickness, the worry. Maybe it's unrealistic to forget the bitter things—but maybe not. I want my daughter to know through my memories that her country welcomed me and gave me a temporary home, and friends who cared about me and about her. And one day, I hope she'll go back to visit again and start to assemble her own photo album. I'd like to go with her.

Being There

I remember arriving. We flew from Tokyo to Beijing to Changsha. I was numb and tired. We landed; I looked out of the 747 and felt I might as well be on the moon. There was a concrete runway broken up in places with grass growing through. People were riding bicycles on the runway. It was all of a sudden so foreign and yet so small-scale, so familiar in a funny way. I thought, I can't believe I've never been here before! It made the world just so small for me. I know that you adopt your child's culture along with your child, but I also believe that intercountry adoption also readjusts the way you feel about connections between people. It alters those deep psychological connections we all have. Here I was on the other side of the world in a place I never thought I'd visit. And people are riding bicycles and it's hot outside and our baby is waiting for us. Something in me changed permanently then.

And now? We're home with our daughter. Mimi opened up a lot of parts of the world for me that hadn't existed before: parenthood, children, . . . China. We want to go back to adopt another child, and possibly a third. But if it works out we have to go elsewhere—well, you have to do what you have to do. Now I have this new sense about traveling. I can't imagine going any other place without adopting a child there! I mean . . . what would you do with yourself? **(RC)**

It was surprising to find that Bogotá, Colombia, was not the "ends of the earth." We stayed in a very nice neighborhood of the city; there were shops, antique stores, art galleries, and so on. There was even a TGI Friday's up the street! We rented an apartment from a wonderful woman who helped us get familiar with Bogotá and even took us on a few day trips.

I felt Bogotá was very safe, even though there were sections of the city I wouldn't visit. Other cities in Colombia have the reputation of being less safe, but still, I would go to Cali or Medellín to adopt. Because a reputable guide or coordinator should know where in the city you can and can't go. You should know ahead of time to what part of the country or to what city you will go, and if you're uncomfortable with that, you can ask for another placement. When you choose a Latin American adoption, you have to be ready for political unrest. That's the reality. That's your choice. If you're afraid, you choose another country to adopt from—Korea, China—or you choose an adoption where you won't have to travel. **(MD)**

I had some Spanish but I wasn't fluent, and what I did have I had to use a lot. I found that exhausting. Everyone in Honduras seemed to talk a million miles an hour. At times listening to my translator and my lawyer talk together, I felt helpless, incompetent. I was totally, utterly dependent on everyone. If they had driven into the center of the city and just dropped me off, I would have been in real trouble! It was a humbling experience and very frustrating. **(PR)**

I felt very comfortable in Korea. The people are very gracious and the streets of Seoul are safe. I got a nice reception from everyone I came into contact with. The hotel I chose wasn't expensive, so I didn't end up in the nicest section of Seoul. But, I stayed in a very colorful part of the city. I got a real flavor of the place.

Getting there was unforgettable. There weren't many people I met that spoke English. Even at Kennedy Airport, there wasn't any English to refer to at all. And even when it was spoken, it was hard to follow.

I got off the airplane . . . and there was all of Seoul. There aren't very many signs (and none in English), so I just followed the crowd. I had to figure out how to get to my hotel and guessed a taxi was the right idea. By mistake I got into the "rip-off" taxi line at the airport, but luckily a woman came along who saw I was a foreigner and asked if I wanted to share a taxi. She spoke broken English, but was very kind. She ushered me into this other taxi line and we got into a cab. We just smiled at each other during the trip into town. She helped me find my hotel and got me dropped off there.

Next, the hotel: no one there spoke any English, either. But I managed to get settled, and then started off to walk to the adoption agency. I had a map of the city. But people in Seoul don't walk across streets when they get to an intersection. Instead, they take stairs down into a massive underground transit system, walk through a tunnel under the street, and back up again. Up and down. The hotel workers persuaded me to take a cab.

Once I got to the agency, I finally found someone I could talk to, because the caseworker spoke English fairly well. After my meeting there, they took me to the orphanage. And after that, I was still pretty much on my own.

I don't consider all of this to be a measure of my bravery, it's just that I often don't think ahead of time what the problems might be. So throughout my stay in South Korea, I felt my way along.

The trip to Seoul went well. But getting back! My daughter had ear infections. And she was eating a lot, so I ended the trip covered with baby food from head to foot. And to top it all off, we ran into bad weather so that it took us ten hours alone to travel from New York to Portland, Maine. We sat in New York, and then we sat in Boston. For hours. And then we spent all this time circling Portland. That was when my tears finally came. There I was, covered with food, exhausted, smelly clothes ... there was nothing left, emotionally, and I knew my family was down there, waiting on the ground.

It's funny. I have pictures of us getting off the plane, but strangely, we look OK. I can't imagine why. After that part of the trip, I can see how some people like the escort programs!   **(FEM)**

I carry a great memory of the roast chicken stand we liked to go to. It was an outdoor operation that took up the whole sidewalk. It opened at dusk. Women stood cooking at open gas burners (it's a wonder we weren't blown to pieces by the gas). There was the smell of cooking meat ... You sat on a rough wooden bench. Buses roared by, trucks raced past practically knocking over the stand.

When we started going there we'd round the corner and they'd see us and start yelling hello! Even after we'd been there only a few times the people always remembered us. They'd hug our baby, chat with us. I remember the way the woman made *picarones* (doughnuts): she'd dip her hand into the batter, shape it, and toss it into the oil. Then she'd serve it with cane sugar. We'd sit on a bench in a row with our friends, passing a plate between us. It didn't seem so special to me then, but I do miss it now. **(FJ)**

I have blond hair and am rather round. So the Chinese looked at me with great curiosity. Some parents found that intimidating. Luckily, I met a woman there who spoke both English and Chinese, and she could tell me what people were saying. Oh, they said, this child is lucky, she's going to heaven. Think of the education she'll have, the opportunities. Some wanted to know if I had a Chinese husband. Some wondered if I was too old to be a mother; was I a grandmother? Every single comment was positive. And I had been worried about that, because I didn't want to be seen as the pompous American who can buy her way through life. **(MEM)**

Our trips to Paraguay were wonderful. The excitement of such a different culture, of knowing how connected we now were to it. And just being in Paraguay, there was a thrill of new adventures, even though they were kind of ordinary. For example, I broke my glasses while we were in Asunción. So one afternoon I went to the optician by myself, walking down the street and repeating over and over the words I knew I'd need for getting across my problem. It sounds funny but I felt so ... grown up, so in control. Such a small thing—but a big deal for me.

We did as much as we could. We love to walk, so we were up and out every day, taking it all in and regretting we couldn't do more. We tried to use all our time wisely; we never sat around. We felt we were information gatherers, so we asked lots of questions—so much that we often got the reply "Why do you want to know that?" We tried not to be rude but we did want to learn as much as we could. With the two kids, we went to Paraguay three times, and with each trip, we knew more and more Spanish. I took a crash course between trips at our local university, and I think it really helped. Knowing the language was important, because Paraguay isn't as connected to the world economy as other places in Latin America and even people in the highest places don't necessarily speak English.

Staying longer would have been nice, but I think with shorter stays, you appreciate every minute; it's easier to focus. At each successive trip, we knew how special it was and how little we had left of it. Our trips were moments in time we didn't really want to let go of. It's funny how much I talk about our involvement with Paraguay, rather than our involvement with being new parents. Of course our children and our new role as parents were our primary excitement, but I felt we could concentrate more on those issues when we got home. While we were in our children's birth country, we were more intent on taking in all we could so that we could have lots to tell and show them later on.

A highlight of our last trip was when our lawyer—by then a very close friend—took us to a family birthday party in a little town outside Asunción. They didn't speak any English, we were stumbling around in Spanish, but it was fascinating and fun to be in a more everyday Paraguayan world. I must have sat there for several hours talking, using our little dictionary. Even though we didn't really get a chance to travel within Paraguay, by meeting people there and visiting with them we felt we did get to know the country. And by having our older daughter with us on our second and third trips, I think we got even more out of Paraguay. We did a lot more things, went to a lot more places because of her. She was given so much attention. Children are well loved there; that's very different from the United States!   **(DE)**

Something that takes getting used to in China is that the boundaries between people are very different. People would walk right up to us in the street, fix Mimi's socks, adjust her hat ...

Cover her! Everyone would say. Chinese children get cold! It was 100 degrees outside, but still, everyone would be very concerned. And I grew to believe it. To this day, I still put two pairs of pajamas on her. My friends laugh at me, but I tell them she needs it—after all, I say, she's Chinese.   **(RC)**

What was most foreign to me in South America was seeing that what men can do and what women can do is so different and so out of balance. Men don't seem to take much responsibility for taking care of and dealing with their children; add to this a poor economy, and it's no wonder that so many children are in need and so many women have no choice but to relinquish them for adoption. The attitude was outrageous sometimes. One day we were in a cab, and my husband got talking to the cabbie. The guy told us he had eight kids. "Wow!" Ray said. "Mucho dinero, no?" The cabbie just shrugged and said no, probably not much. Like it wasn't his concern. I couldn't believe it. There he was boasting about how many kids he had, but he didn't even seem to know how much it took to support them! His kids' quality of life didn't seem to be any big deal to him. We were told that late at night (Paraguayans are up till all hours of the night—that was quite different), a few blocks from our hotel, we'd find dozens of kids begging in the streets. Nobody feels they have any direct responsibility toward them, not even the government. There's no tax structure in Paraguay, and therefore no social programs. Maybe if the government doesn't recognize the need, people in turn don't think they should, either. The culture somehow doesn't teach a sense of social responsibility.   **(WK)**

O ur son got sick while we were in Peru. At first I wasn't worried— he had a bit of diarrhea, but was still eating well. But when it got worse, we finally asked the hotel manager to telephone a doctor for us. We got an appointment for late in the day.

We took a cab to this dilapidated building and sat with the baby in a tired old waiting room with a bunch of other people. Finally, we were shown into an examining room where the doctor shuffled in, looking as if he had just stepped away from his dinner to take a look at this little patient. We managed to explain to him in our miserable Spanish about the diarrhea, and he proceeded to give our baby the roughest exam I've ever seen. He poked and prodded until I thought my husband would punch him out. We were about to snatch our son away and leave, but then the doctor sat down and wrote us out a prescription for some medicine at the local drugstore. He slowly explained what we would need to do to keep the baby comfortable, then reached behind him and came up with a packet of medicine to dissolve in water for the baby's bottle.

We thanked the doctor, paid him, dressed our son and hurried out of there as fast as we could. We were still angry about the examination and wanted to get as far from his office as we could. Oh, well. At least he had given us a prescription and we could start fixing up some medication right away with the stuff he had given us. Back at the hotel, I finally took a closer look at the medicine.

It was a packet of UNICEF oral rehydration salts. The kind that I knew saved babies' lives in far off countries in Africa and Asia. And in

Peru. I remembered the pennies for UNICEF I had collected each Halloween when I was little, and all the pictures of starving kids and sad-looking babies from the UNICEF brochures that came with the collection boxes. Never in my wildest dreams did I imagine those pennies would end up back in my hands.

We bought more medicine at the drugstore, and the diarrhea went away in the next few days. We went home several weeks later. I threw away all our half-finished bottles of drugs from Peru soon after we saw our pediatrician for our son's first U.S. checkup.

But I'll keep that half-empty packet of rehydration salts for a long, long time. **(LVP)**

Yes, I'd do it all again. I'd do it in a minute. Despite the fact that I was living away from home, on my own with a brand-new baby, how many people can say that they were able to spend such a long, uninterrupted amount of time with their children and not have to worry about all the other stuff in life? I felt that was very, very special. Of course it was especially hard not to be able to have my friends and family know Hannah as an infant—she was over eight months when I brought her home. But it's just as hard now to be separated from the beginnings of our life together. I can remember every street I walked with Hannah, all the sights and smells and sounds of Miraflores and San Isidro in Lima. I wish I could have brought it all home with me, somehow. I have a craving for that time in my life, and for the people of Peru, for the culture. I mourn the sadness of the country, its poverty, Hannah's birthmother, the unfairness of the haves and the have-nots of this world. And I desperately wish for my ties to Peru, Hannah's ties, to stay alive.

(TS)

Jean's Journal

July 2, 1990

Dear Jessie,

Katie and Debbie and Terry have all left Iquitos, and you and I are the American outpost here for a while. Or I am, anyway.

Iquitos is geographically larger than I had thought; and because no building goes above about four stories and most of the houses are simple structures with thatched roofs, often built on stilts above the river or on rafts actually on the water, it sprawls in many directions. The Amazon River itself is about a quarter of a mile from the *hostal*; a mere two miles wide here at its source, people assure me that downstream it becomes *really* wide, so wide you cannot see across it. There is a town square with exquisitely flowering trees, a statue honoring military veterans (though no one can tell me of what conflict), and a waterless fountain depicting the pink freshwater dolphin they say lives in the Amazon. The major Catholic church, also on the Plaza de Armas, is quite large with a stucco front wall and a bell tower; its roof is corrugated metal. The church bells are rung by hand to announce the services; when I heard them yesterday, I took you there for the padre's blessing.

Prospero Street is the main commercial street in town, and so far as I can tell, about the only street that is paved from one end to the other. Except for a couple of banks and an office of Aeroperu, it is lined with little shops and sidewalk vendors, which become more numerous as Prospero leads into the Belén market. Belén is an area of thatched buildings and houses on stilts and rafts, and seems from a distance as desperately poor as anything I have ever seen; I would like to visit Belén, but they tell me in the *hostal* that I should not go alone. I remember my early geography lesson about the Amazon, which said that the "Indians" lived in large structures shared by many families; at least here, I see no evidence of this at all, but the many thatched roofs, so close together that they often touch, might give this impression from a distance. I wonder if this is one of the many misapprehensions sent back as fact by colonialists and early missionaries, who tried to describe what they thought they saw without much troubling themselves to understand it.

After staying awake all night our first night together, the dawn brought a stream of phone calls to and from the States. I was, in fact, calling out on one phone when my sister and brother-in-law called in on another. This is all the more remarkable because long-distance phone service is intermittent at best. Everyone wants to know about you: "Do you have the baby?" "What is she like?" "How big is she?" "Does she have hair?" Even by long-distance telephone, I can hear their excitement. I suppose they want to know how I am too, but this seems to be fairly far down on the lists of their questions.

Our first day and second night together were tense for both of us. You ate ravenously, then slept almost immediately thereafter, so we had only a little time to get to know each other. But today is different—the people at the *hostal* desk and dining room confirm my impression that you are more alert to things and people around you. They also confirm what I could not really believe: that at four weeks old you have at least one, and possibly two teeth! The women say it means you are very advanced, but when I talked to Wong on the phone, he said it means only that you have teeth.

This morning I met with the social worker, Nancy, and Maria—a legal requirement after which the social worker must report that your biological mother understands the implications of her surrender of you for adoption and has been under no coercion to do so. Maria said little at this meeting, and spoke very softly, but sometimes I could see her eyes fill with tears. Although there is a long tradition here of having one's children raised by members of the extended family, giving you to a total stranger must be incredibly difficult for her.

After our meeting, we all piled into *motocarros* and went to visit your foster mother, Rosalita, and her family in their apartment just off Prospero Street. Her apartment is small and simply furnished, and deliberately kept dark to resist the tropical sun that beats down with a fury at midday. Rosalita showed me how she fed you a paste of bananas and formula; she says this paste is very filling, and helps to stabilize the digestive system. Rosalita held you so lovingly as she fed you, and cried as she rocked you back and forth while her five-year-old daughter stroked your black hair and gave you a bottle. She said that she has cared for many children, but that you are special.

As I sit here now, rocking you in a wicker rocker on one of the landings of the *hostal*, catching whatever breezes blow at midday, I am so grateful for the sweet and generous time you knew in Rosalita's little apartment. It assures me that you will never in your life have known anyone who did not love you.

July 3

Dear Jessie,

Today was more difficult. The little cough you had when you arrived has developed into a full-fledged illness, so last night we went to see one of the two pediatricians in town. The doctor's office was tiny and virtually without medical equipment: an examining table, a few charts on the wall, a scale, and a stethoscope. But how kindly and carefully he measured you (forty-nine centimeters) and weighed you (plus or minus eight pounds) and listened to your chest! He told me you are underweight, and that the banana paste Rosalita gave you is commonly fed to babies here to fill their stomachs when a mother has insufficient breast milk or formula. That is probably why, fever or no fever, you are hungry all the time!

The doctor prescribed for you antibiotic injections, and a decongestant. Because electricity is so erratic in Peru, any medication requiring refrigeration is kept either in the hospital or in pharmacies with auxiliary power. So Alex and I walked to a pharmacy where we bought individual doses of the antibiotic, along with the needles and syringes required for injection; then we took you to the hospital clinic, a storefront kind of place, where a nurse gave you the medication. Your doctor called the *hostal* early this morning to see how you are, and I am reassured that the absence of high technology is compensated for by the careful concern of this pediatrician.

We had a sleepless night until the medication took hold. Then, this morning, I learned from Alex and Dr. A that a local newsperson asserted last night on television news that babies are being bought and sold here in Iquitos. Because the only visible Americans in town recently have been Katie, Debbie and Terry, and I, all of us carrying babies, he evidently referred to our *hostal* by name. My first reaction is pure terror. I know I must do something, anything, to prevent even the possibility of having to give you back.

So after Alex and I took you for your second injection, we went to visit Father J, the primary cleric in town who is also the editor of the newspaper. It was he who first learned that a Peruvian woman (definitely not Charo, who is back in the States) was arrested here a few days or weeks ago for giving mothers money for their infants and then taking them secretly out of Iquitos. Alex tells me that Father J is highly respected by many people, and it is important that he know *my* story too. As we sat on hard chairs in front of his desk, I started to tell it in my stumbling Spanish and to fish out my documents and letters of introduction. After a few moments Father J stopped me. It seems that he was the padre who blessed you last Sunday morning at the *catedral*. He said he knows that no one would have brought for a public blessing a child she had stolen. He shook my hand warmly, and said he would see that any rumors about me ended.

By the time Alex and I had returned to the *hostal*, there was a phone call from the local television station. At Father J's request, they wanted to interview me in response to the adoption story. They agreed to come to the *hostal*, and asked me to bring to the interview any official papers I have to document my legitimacy. Dr. A and Alex selected: my foster parent license from the State of Illinois; the Interpol clearance documenting that I have no record as an international criminal; and (God bless them!) my letters of introduction from Monsignor E, Bishop G, and Senator D. In order to be sure that there are no misunderstandings because of language, I agreed to speak only English and let Alex translate. The interview went quite smoothly, and the camera showed you several times sleeping peacefully in my lap. Then, just at the end, they asked me one question they believed I could answer without a translator: Had I given anyone money to purchase my baby? I answered emphatically, "No."

In spite of these rumors, somehow I feel safe here, wrapped almost in a cocoon. I feel so fortunate to have such wonderful support, from Dr. A (who, after what we've just been through, believes I am entitled to call him by his familiar name, Quique), from Alex, and from all the people who work at the *hostal*. And as long as I'm with you, I am at home. We have been together only four days, and yet I am struck already by something a new mother once said to me years ago: that before she had her child, she couldn't imagine having a baby in her life, but once her son was born, she couldn't imagine her life without him. I cannot imagine my life anymore without you, and I know that I will do whatever I must to keep you, now that, at long last, I have the right Jessie.

July 4

Dear Jessie,

We stayed close to home all day today as you recover from your cold and we allow some time for rumors to die away. We are more than comfortable in the *hostal*, almost more comfortable than we would be in Chicago. Though it is blazingly hot, especially during siesta from 12:30 to 4:00, our room is air-conditioned, and there is a tiny swimming pool in the courtyard. When our clothes are dirty, someone comes and takes them away, and they return almost magically the next day, all washed and folded. When I am hungry, we can either go to the little *hostal* dining room or have food brought to us. I am eating a steady diet of *paiche*, a sweet white fish indigenous to the Amazon River, with side orders of fried *plátanos*. I will probably be the only *gringa* on record who comes back from South America fatter than when she left.

I look at you for hours at a time, sleeping peacefully on my stomach. You are so clearly your own little person already. That you cry real tears surprises me; I suppose I didn't expect your cries from hunger or discomfort to be attached yet to real emotion. I find myself wondering what is already going on behind your dark eyes, what you dream about when you stir in your sleep. We've even had our first little fight—a power struggle really, between a grown woman and a month-old baby, over your pacifier. Although you take your "nuk" when it is offered, and it does quiet your crying, as soon as I move my finger, you *phtt*! spit it out. Last night, quite late, you cried and cried for no reason I could discern. Afraid that you would disturb our neighbors here in the *hostal*, I gave you the nuk, and you spat it out. Again and again we did this, until finally I simply held it there as I stood over your crib, explaining to you that while we may be equally stubborn, I have forty-plus years of practice at it so I would probably outlast you. After I had stood there a long time, my eyes drifted shut, my finger slipped, and *phtt*! out came the nuk. But by then, you were asleep. I'd say our first quarrel was a draw.

The *hostal* receives cable television, and from time to time I can get CNN on the TV in our room. It is Independence Day at home, and I am mildly amused to hear about how hot it is back in the States—no one knows hot until they've been in Iquitos! At intervals, reporters are doing random interviews with Americans in various parts of the country about how they plan to spend this hot holiday. And suddenly, there on the television screen is Chicago's Oak Street beach, and there, on the Oak Street beach, are two people from my choir, talking about going to the movies and then cooking hot dogs with friends. For a moment, it is almost as though I have never left home.

As I reflect on this remarkable coincidence, I am startled by how small this world is becoming. During my homestudy, I told Julie that we would probably have a graduate student from the university live in with us to help with child care. But now, I am more than ever determined to try to find a child-care person to help me raise you bilingually. I think we should make a pact with her (or him, I suppose) that the three of us will only speak Spanish together. Even if you eventually do not speak much Spanish as a child, at least you will have a foundation that may help you learn your native language more fluently later, if you decide you want to.

I think it will be a good thing for both of us to know Spanish. The world is even smaller than I had thought: you can see the Oak Street beach from the Amazon River.

July 5

Dear Jessie,

You were much better today, and Quique (Tio Quique, I suppose) suggested I get a babysitter and get out of the *hostal* for a while. So with Alex's guidance (and Alex knows *everyone* in Iquitos), I hired a guide and boat and went with Quique up the river. We told the guide we wanted to see something *real* (or as close to real as tourists can see anyway). After several hours on the boat, we hiked for about an hour in the jungle looking at various plants and animals, until we came to a tiny village. Actually, the village was just four or five thatched houses on stilts within sight of one another. The men were gone, probably fishing, our guide said; there isn't much hunting left in this part of the jungle. Bare-breasted women and naked children greeted us shyly, the children's bellies swollen from hunger and intestinal parasites.

For an American like me, this visit was *National Geographic* come to life. But it was more than a sight to be seen. It gave me a small sense of how traditional life in the jungle has been disrupted by the destruction of the rain forest, of how the intrusion of civilization that brought Quique and me for a visit has created the kind of massive social dislocation that drives thousands of people out of the jungle to struggle for survival in thatched huts on the edge of places like Iquitos. I was saddened by the poverty I saw in the village, of course; they say it was not always so. But I am sadder still to know that the way of life I glimpsed today, and what these simple people know about the mysteries of the rain forest, may be for you what it has until now been for me . . . the stuff of magazine stories.

For even so far from civilization as we were today, we were never away from the distant sound of the chainsaws.

July 6

Dearest daughter,

Today, I took legal custody of you in a brief paper signing at the courthouse. Once again, I had *mariposas en el estómago*. This was the moment when the mother of another child, in Paraguay, suddenly knew she could not part with her infant daughter. And with the rumors that have been flying, who knew what could happen?

Quique, who has decided not to commute back and forth between Iquitos and his family in Lima but to stay here and take care of us, has been nervously planning how to deal with the rumors if they do not subside. Alex has heard that Maria's grandmother is evidently afraid Maria has done something illegal. So we invited Maria to come to the *hostal* yesterday to visit you. I gave her pictures of our house and your nursery, and I told her about all the people waiting so anxiously back in the States for us to come home. She promised she would tell her grandmother. I realized for the first time after this visit that Maria may very well not have much support from her family for this decision to give you away. What extraordinary courage this must take!

After the papers were signed, we all went to lunch at a restaurant on stilts above the Amazon. It seems a bit fancier than other places in town, and I wanted to go there because I suspect Maria will never get to go to Maloka again. During lunch, Alex helped me talk with Maria about your biological family.

Maria herself is twenty-seven years old. She said she has a year or two of secondary school, but I have seen her try to write and doubt that she is more than barely literate; she had to quit school when she became pregnant for the first time. Maria has two other children, approximately seven and five years old, a boy and a girl; she has never been married. She was born in Nauta, a small town not far from here along the river; her other children are there now with her parents. About a year ago, Maria left Nauta and came to Iquitos to live with an aunt while she looked for work. Instead, she met your father, a "student," who disappeared when he learned she was pregnant; I will try at least to find out his name for you. At first, Maria's aunt said she would help her take care of you, but by the time you were born, no one in that house had work anymore and so the aunt could not take you either. Maria said she had a healthy, easy pregnancy with you, and that you were born in her aunt's home in a hammock, attended by a midwife.

I am slowly coming to understand how central the concept of family is in this culture. What makes it different from the American idea seems to have something to do with the primacy of children; they may be born legitimately or illegitimately, but once they are here, one relative or another usually steps forward to care for them when the mother cannot. Thus, in contrast to our comparatively tidy one- or two-parent families with their immediate children, families here are mixes of generations and lines. Alex was raised by his grandparents; Theresita, our dear young friend who teaches me how to take care of you, grew up in the home of a distant aunt; and Marisa, who works at the *hostal*'s front desk, has a two-year-old who lives in Lima with her parents while she and her husband are here, holding the only jobs they can find in an economy with 30 percent unemployment. And thus, Maria's other children live with her parents in another town, and her grandmother takes the decision to give you up for adoption as personally as if it were her own.

Perhaps I will be able to learn more about Maria and her family and background after I have been here a while and she has had more opportunities to visit and become comfortable with me. But it is hard to know how much to ask without being intrusive. Katie had a wonderful idea that I'm sorry I didn't think of. She gave Cristina's biological mother a small tape player with a record function and some blank tapes, and asked her to tell Cristina through the tape recorder whatever she wants her child to know one day. This seems to me to answer a child's need to know while at the same time respecting the biological mother's and family's privacy. And what an extraordinary gift to Cristina!

In a world where Maria and her family have so little, surely we can give them that: respect.

July 7

Dear Jessie,

Last night and early this morning were hard again. After Theresita and I had done all we could to comfort you, at noon we called the pediatrician, who made a *hostal* call. Your congestion continues, irritated by what appears to be active teething. The teething is made worse by some sort of oral fungus; everything is so alive here that it would almost surprise me if we didn't have some fungus or parasite between us. I have learned that the refrigerator in our room is both for keeping things cold and for keeping them away from the almost invisible wildlife around us; I refrigerate everything—clean nipples, pacifiers, your medications and droppers, even my toothbrush.

In the middle of last night, as you cried inconsolably, I found myself wondering if I had indeed bitten off more than I can chew by becoming a single parent. But then in the morning the people of the *hostal* began to come to our door, asking what they could do to help. Theresita came to hold and rock you several times while I napped briefly. When you cried so hard that I couldn't hear the doctor explaining the medications he'd prescribed, Tio Alex and Manuel scooped up little toys and rattles and took you off together, dancing and singing and calling out, "Jesusita, Jesusita!" Later, they both flew around in *motocarros* to find the prescriptions you need. No pharmacy, it seems, has them all.

Gradually, I am learning about the compensations that come with single parenting. True enough, last night there was no one to help me hold you and rock you, no one to hold and rock me as you cried so in my arms. But today, I am aware that many, many people have offered their help to us just in the last few hours. I wonder if they would feel as free to make such offers if I were here with a partner, even a partner who could or would do nothing to help with a tiny baby. Or would they make the assumption that adoption is a private affair between a man and a woman, and something into which outsiders should not intrude without specific invitation? I suspect the community of adoptive aunts and uncles waiting at home for you might not be so vast, and their eagerness to embrace you as their own more guarded, if I were married.

This afternoon, after you started your new prescriptions, we both slept a deep, refreshing sleep, and woke in time for a pleasant supper with Tio Quique. He says that next week it would be good to have a fiesta and invite the judge's clerks for a nice lunch here at the *hostal*. Bureaucrats at every level are paid poorly here, and like waiters and waitresses in the States who work for minimum wage, they depend heavily on the side fees and gifts they collect (hence, the gifts Charo suggested I bring with me). To most Americans, this looks like bribery, but it really is more like "leaving a tip" for services rendered. Quique says the need for everyone to get his or her fee is part of why the system of adoption in Lima is so slow and cumbersome.

Instead of giving money and gifts, Quique thinks that I should entertain, give little parties, as an expression of my appreciation to officials who help me. He says these fiestas should not be elaborate, but rather simple invitations to dine with me at my Iquitos "home." Unlike in most of the United States, business in much of the Third World is done through relationships; I am glad Quique has helped me find a way to establish a personal contact with those on whose good will I depend. It will give me a chance to learn more about Peru and Iquitos, and to share my adoption story so that the officials here will know I have come here honestly. Quique doesn't say this, but I suspect he also thinks this will help dampen any effects that the rumors of last week may have had.

You seem to like the idea too. You always seem happiest when we are walking and rocking in a place where there are other people. Even at night, you prefer to be rocked as I walk the tiled hallways (I will be able to reproduce the tile pattern in my mind for the rest of my life) over being shut away in our room with just your mother for entertainment. Monday morning we will go to Prospero Street and buy you some party dresses, so you can enter the social whirl we are about to create here in the Amazon.

July 8

Dear Jessie,

The *hostal* is filled with Americans; it seems this is a place where Amazon River boat tours sometimes assemble. You and I are the "old hands" here, and everyone wants to know about you and about my adventure here in Peru. We pose for lots of pictures; these Americans see, as I do, that you are adorable. There are substantially fewer tourists than were expected this year in Peru, a harsh blow for little Iquitos, which had hoped for a boom in tourism along the Amazon River. People read about the narcotics trade, the Sendero Luminoso or "Shining Path" guerrillas, the political instability. There are easier places to go on vacation.

The Americans who are here express such admiration for my courage in coming to Peru, in being here, alone (though I am hardly alone with Quique, Alex, and all our friends here at the *hostal*). Perhaps. But what strikes me as a *real* example of courage are Terry and Debbie, who had never been on an airplane until the day they flew to Peru to adopt a baby. There are many other families like them, truly courageous people with little exposure to cities, let alone foreign cultures in the Third World, who adopt internationally because it is their best hope of becoming parents. Like foreigners anywhere, many of them experience lost wallets and stolen passports, though I have heard of no one who has been the victim of violence. Gradually, I understand another dimension of what I saw among the American families in Lima, a kind of fortress mentality I often see in the States among students who have come to the city to attend the university.

I see now how easy it would be, if there were more Americans here with me, day after day sharing the experience of becoming parents in a faraway place, to become isolated among ourselves, supporting one another as best we could. Yes, I have to admit it would be a great relief to be able to ask someone besides Quique and Alex about your diaper rash, and to do it in English at that. And it would be easier to move in groups to look at Iquitos and shop at the markets, easier still to stay in the *hostal* and interact with one another rather than with Peruvians. Though there are clearly places in Iquitos I do not go as a single woman, I have felt welcome almost everywhere I have gone with my baby and my paperback dictionary; as part of a group, it would be easier on both sides to keep at a distance from each other. Such distances breed misunderstandings, and misunderstandings feed fear. And even among the bravest of us, fear is just below the surface.

Today, as we often do, you and I were sitting on the tile steps of the *hostal* around noon watching the children on their way home from school. Among the children ten-year-old Manuelito is our buddy, and he tells us many things that Peruvian children know. For example, he tells us that other Peruvians call the people of Iquitos *charapos*, mud turtles, because of their slow and unhurried ways. The people of Iquitos are insulted by this, although they themselves call their children *charapitos*, little mud turtles. Manuelito calls you *Jesusita charapita*, Little Jesus Girl the Mud Turtle.

When he stopped this afternoon, Manuelito was very serious. He wanted to ask me something: "Are you that baby's mother?"

I said I was.

"But did the baby come from *your* tummy? Are you her *real* mother?" he asked.

I told him that you were adopted, and that I am your *real* mother now.

"What is that, `adopted?'" he wanted to know, with a serious and what suddenly seemed to be a stern expression in his eyes.

I felt my heart beat faster. Dear God, were the rumors of baby selling so widespread that even the children of Iquitos have heard them? Has even little Manuelito learned to distrust me?

I told him carefully that your first mother, the mother from whose tummy you came, was not able to take care of you, and that she had asked me to be your mother now. I told him we went to the courthouse, and the judge there said this would be all right.

Manuelito nodded sagely and retired a few steps to share his newfound expertise about being "adopted" with some friends. In a few minutes he returned, smiling broadly.

He and his friends were most relieved, he said, to know about being "adopted." "We think you are very pretty," he went on, "but we were pretty sure you were too old to be a mommy."

Distances breed misunderstandings, and misunderstandings feed fear. And sometimes when fear is suddenly relieved, we laugh till we cry.

July 12

Dear Jessie,

A day of big events. We had our first power failure since my arrival in Iquitos. *Problemas en la planta*, a generator station that is old, overtaxed, and poorly maintained. Life, however, goes on pretty much as usual in town. Larger businesses, including the banks and those few enterprises with electronic equipment, have gasoline-powered auxiliary generators—noisy and smelly things, but they keep the lights on. The storefront shops and the merchants on Prospero Street do business by the light of day, as always. Tonight, I write this entry by flashlight.

A mix-up between Quique and me almost delayed the signing of the next phase of adoption papers by a week; the *fiscal* (who is something like a state's attorney) seems only to do business, or at least this kind of business, on one afternoon a week. There was much excitement and flying around in *motocarros*, but we made the deadlines before siesta. After we'd eaten a light lunch, Quique and Alex went out for a walk together followed by well-earned naps.

Without air-conditioning, one understands easily the custom of siesta in this climate. You and I had just settled down for our own nap when the telephone rang. Marisa, at the desk, told me that the *abuelita* was here. What *abuelita*? Marisa didn't know. The older woman who was waiting near the reception desk had simply said to tell me the *abuelita* was here. I went downstairs confused, but the moment I saw Maria standing beside a tiny, ageless woman, I knew: this was Maria's grandmother, the woman who has had such misgivings about your adoption. Maria said shyly that her grandmother had insisted on coming. I could feel my stomach begin to churn. We were on our own: no Quique, no Alex to translate, just you, me, and my paperback dictionary.

I invited them to our room where you were stirring to wakefulness, as if you knew you had better perform, and perform well. The *abuelita* held you briefly and examined your teeth approvingly; she, too, said that early teeth mean you are very advanced. You smiled at her appreciatively so she could see them better. Then, while Maria gave you a bottle, I showed your great-grandmother pictures of your future home and family. She seemed especially touched by all the little dresses I've bought for you so that you will have something from Iquitos to wear on every birthday until you are five. At first, the *abuelita* was very cautious, almost stern; but the thing I had feared she would most disapprove, that I am adopting you as a single parent, seemed not to bother her at all. Slowly, she began to tell me that this was a sad time for her family. She herself has had twelve children, eight girls and four boys, one of whom is Maria's father and your grandfather. There has never before been a child born to this extended family that they could not find a way to care for somehow. While the *abuelita* is finally persuaded from our television appearance, the pictures and messages I sent with Maria last week, and this visit that the adoption is legal, she knew she had to meet me, to know me and talk to me, before she could let you go with a sense of peace. She has a permanent home in Iquitos, *and* a telephone, and Maria wrote the address and phone number on a page of my journal so that we will always have a way of keeping contact with them. I took a picture of the three of you together; I will send copies back to the *abuelita*'s address and will frame one for your nursery.

When Quique returned to the *hostal* from his nap, I told him with great excitement that the *abuelita* had come to visit. He grew suddenly pale: Why hadn't I tried to call him? Didn't I know that he had stayed in Iquitos to take care of me on just such occasions as this? I suppose I should have tried to reach him, but at the time it seemed disrespectful to be unwilling to meet with your biological mother and great-grandmother without a lawyer present. They do, after all, have a right to visit you and to know what will become of the child they have given to me. So I had crossed my fingers and hoped this could be what it in fact was, just a visit among family. But Quique was very agitated: How do I know that the *abuelita* did not leave here intent on fueling the baby-selling rumors? Because, I told him, she has invited my baby and me home for supper. Of her four sons, several are unmarried, and one is quite tall, and she thought it would be nice for me to meet them. And then she kissed us both. Even Quique could smile at this. We both know this meeting without him could have been disastrous if the *abuelita* had not much cared for me. I bought him a large whiskey at supper.

I liked the *abuelita* very much, and I am very glad to know her. I will always remember her dignity, her values, and the sense of her responsibility to you, which brought her uninvited to our *hostal* to meet and measure the woman who would take her great-grandchild away from the jungle forever. I see now where Maria has gotten the courage to make the difficult decision to give you up and the strength to see it through. The *abuelita* reminded me a little of my Aunt Jennie, after whom you are partly named; not very far beneath the strength and the dignity there is also warmth and humor and affection, the same qualities that are more obvious in Maria. One day I will tell you about this extraordinary visit, and about how seriously the decision to give you up for adoption was made by many members of your biological family. We will find a way to stay in touch with the *abuelita* so that someday we can come back to Iquitos and accept her invitation to supper.

Finally tonight, one last event. The power continues to flicker on and off, and our part of Iquitos is completely dark. It was Alex who came to our door a little while ago with a flashlight and a flan from a little bar on the plaza. You were sleeping soundly, and he asked me to join him on the roof. We climbed the stairs to the top floor of the *hostal* and then up a little ladder until we reached the tile roof. And when I looked up, what I saw took my breath away.

All the twinkling lights and traffic noises that I am accustomed to in cities were gone. In their place, a blanket of stars like none I had ever seen before arched across the still night. A few birds sang, nothing more. And I knew with certainty that to be in this place, and at long last with my daughter, is nothing short of a miracle.

July 13

Dearest Jessie,

Today, we had another fiesta to honor the judge and the *fiscal*. We invited their families, and then we decided to invite the law clerks and their families too. And when so many people were already coming, I decided to invite our friends here at the *hostal* as well. Alex took care of everything, and the people who work in the kitchen and dining room, honored to have been included, outdid themselves. We had fish and *plátanos* and *chicharrones de pollo*, little pieces of chicken fried in a light batter and served with various dipping sauces (Alex says they are the Peruvian version of Chicken McNuggets). We even found some wine in a local store, to supplement the more commonly served beer. Alex set the tables out around the little courtyard swimming pool, and borrowed some of my tapes for background music. I had long talks with both the judge and the *fiscal*, and they both posed for pictures with you in one of your new party dresses. From time to time I also overheard Quique and Alex in conversation with them, extolling my virtues as an *excelente persona*.

When the guests of honor had left, those of us still at the *hostal*, heavy with food and beer and wine in the tropical midday, settled back for a chat. Wine in the middle of the day gave me the courage finally to ask my Peruvian friends where the idea of baby selling comes from here, and why people so readily believe it. First, they told me that even in legitimate adoptions some money changes hands: just as in the States, biological mothers usually receive a small, carefully calculated sum to cover the expenses of their pregnancy and child care before the child is surrendered. But sometimes biological fathers hear about this and begin to insist on their own rights to payment; other times, honorable people like the *abuelita* become concerned when suddenly a mother has extra cash and no child. And there are always a few unscrupulous people (like the woman the *padre* reported on last week) who do in fact pay mothers outright for their children, bargaining for them as if they were cars in a showroom. Foreigners who are anxious, even desperate, to become parents are sometimes willing to pay extra for a quick and easy adoption process and a healthy child. I know the temptation I would have felt myself a few months ago if someone had offered me a speedy, uncomplicated placement, though I know that such a placement would never have come with the rich experiences of knowing your family that I have had. I also understand now why both Charo and Quique insisted on documenting your surrender in photographs, and why they have told me repeatedly to refer anyone who mentions the payment of money to them.

I was also told that Peruvians have heard that Americans come here to buy children to be servants, prostitutes, even the victims of medical experimentation back in the States. Why on earth would anyone believe that? Because children who are surrendered for adoption are usually from the lower classes of this society, and the lower classes are often racially darker than people of the middle and upper classes. Some Peruvians simply cannot believe that prosperous fair-skinned Americans would come here to make these dark, frequently Indian-looking children their own. This must be why it seemed so important to the *abuelita* to see pictures of your new home and waiting family, why she seemed so touched by all the little dresses I had bought. I gave her some photos to keep, and I imagine her showing them to her family and friends as evidence that her great-granddaughter indeed went home as part of my family. I wish I had given her and Maria even more pictures of places and people; I will make a point of sending these to them in the future.

Much though I have hated the red tape of the international adoption process, I now understand at least in part why it exists. The only way to prevent these abuses from happening, even becoming commonplace as they once were in Southeast Asia, is to make the process of acquiring, processing, and taking a child out of one country and into another as non-cost-effective as possible. The honest and loving people I have met here who are becoming parents pay the price of this. But as the days and weeks roll on here in Peru, it is a help at least to know why.

July 14

My dear child,

And so this bright Saturday noon, without warning, the clerks of the adoption court arrived on bicycles with the final *sentencia*, the decree of adoption. It was signed yesterday by the judge and the *fiscal* this morning. The decree will be filed in the Iquitos courthouse on Monday morning and then, after three days and just short of three weeks from the day you first came to me, we are free to go home. The adoption is final and irrevocable: insofar as any person belongs to another, you belong to me. You are my daughter, Jessie Victoria Maria.

For the rest of my life, I will remember the faces of Tio Quique and Tio Alex when they first saw the decree. First, Quique, as he realized he will have pulled off an adoption in less than three weeks. Surprised, proud of himself, happy for us, he went chortling around the *hostal* mumbling to himself, "Three weeks . . . ha, ha, ha, three weeks . . . " When Alex arrived, we didn't tell him what the document was, only that I would like for him to read it to me in English. He read carefully the names of all the parties, the dates of the intervening decrees, then stopped suddenly at the last paragraph: "This is it?" he shouted; "Dios mio, Jean, this is it!" That was when I burst into tears.

If there was ever excuse for a party, we had one today. Quique thought we should go dancing. So we gathered together the court clerks who have become the staple of our parties, "Miss Iquitos" who is staying at the *hostal* after winning a beauty pageant, and anyone else who was free this warm Saturday afternoon, and went to a place called *Las Gaviotas* (The Seagulls) where a live rock band plays from midday until midnight Saturday and Sunday. We danced and we danced: Quique and I, Alex and I, Quique and Alex and I. And then we danced with others. I danced with a beautiful little girl, Yuly, who had lost her two front teeth; I told her my baby had found them. At Alex's request, the band played something called "La Chica de Chicago," and our entire adoption party danced together in a circle. We danced until we were spent, then went back to the *hostal* to pick you up and head to Maloka for supper.

As I watch you now, sleeping peacefully in our little borrowed crib, feelings sweep over me in waves. I think of all the years ahead of us, and I remind myself that you are already your own little person, not my creation or invention and certainly not my belonging. I think about all the women for whom you are named: the first Jessie Knoll, my grandmother, my mother Jean, and my aunt Jen. And now, after me, there is another Jessie. I think about Maria and the *abuelita* and wonder how their lives will be and what part we will play in them. And I wonder who you will become, and what you will give to the world, and how much of your life I will live to see. I wish my parents were still alive to bring you home to; whatever their misgivings might have been, there is something miraculous about any baby, and something even more miraculous about you.

My life is unalterably changed now. I've been on my own for too long. I think that over the years alone I grew, not hard exactly, but increasingly disconnected from my feelings. The soft and gentle parts of my soul were eclipsed by bright energy and quiet ambition. There were fewer and fewer places where I let those parts of me be seen, and if I kept busy enough, fewer and fewer times when I even confronted them myself. I noticed some time this spring that I hardly ever cry anymore, even in private.

Today, dear daughter, I cried. And then . . . I danced!

July 17

Dear Jessie,

Against Quique's advice, Tio Alex and I hired a *motocarro* this afternoon and tried to find the house where you were born. The adoption decree gave an address and described it as *de condición humilde*, of humble character. According to the decree, it is built of wood, with a corrugated metal roof and a cement floor. It has three rooms: a living room, a bedroom, and a kitchen, and there is a small garden. There are hundreds, if not thousands, of houses like this on the edge of Iquitos. Most often they begin as what we in the States call "squatters' settlements," vacant land on which the people who come into town from the *selva* (rain forest) or the *chacra* (farmlands) build temporary and then more permanent shelter on land nobody really owns. They rarely have plumbing or electricity.

Our *motocarro* traveled past dozens of poor, simple houses on Ricardo Palma Road until it finally ended in a dirt path. Houses went on down that path as far as we could see, and I imagine one of them was the house of Maria's aunt. Alex and I decided not to go any farther. To drive quickly past a house is one thing, but to walk to it deliberately, past neighbors and friends, seemed intrusive somehow of Maria's right to privacy. Intrusive of her dignity too, because the poverty in those houses is quite desperate. I am sorry I cannot tell you more, but I want very much to leave with Maria and her family the sense of our respect for them, and of our deepest gratitude.

July 19

Dear Jessie,

Tonight, as I lie here waiting for you to wake up and demand, oh, so insistently, your right to a bottle, I am surrounded by suitcases packed for our long trip home. Except for the crib, the room looks as it did almost exactly three weeks ago when you came into my life. Odd, to think that it could be the same when everything else in my world and yours is different now. I think of this room as a kind of cocoon in which we learned to live together, almost untouched by the real world.

Tomorrow we begin the reentry process, and in a few days you will be the *chica de Chicago* and our life in the real world will begin. Charo and Tio Quique and Tio Alex and Theresita will remain a part of our lives for a long time; our Chicago family is waiting eagerly. Wong, in fact, has canceled all his surgical responsibilities for two days so that he can be at the airport whenever we arrive; Tia Felisa (formerly, Phyllis) will get the word of our arrival out. I suspect we shall have quite a gathering when our plane arrives, and a steady flow of relatives and friends after that, all eager to meet you (and to see me again too, I suppose). But while I look forward to that, some part of me is also sad: sad to leave the good people here at the *hostal* who have befriended us; sad to leave Iquitos, even though I think we've done everything there is to do here except meet a pink dolphin; and sad to leave this interesting and desperately troubled country without having left something behind to help. This is the best way for this journey to end: to be sad to leave and enormously grateful to the wonderful people who have given you to me.

We also went to the *padre* today, you and I, to ask for his blessing as we leave Iquitos and to give a small donation to the sisters who care for abandoned children here. My beautiful new daughter is a child of Iquitos too, who, but for the grace of God, may well have been abandoned to the sisters' care. As you grow up, I will teach you that we share a responsibility to the children we leave behind here, and especially to those who are too old or too sick ever to be adopted by anyone.

Tonight, as I packed the little pink dress you arrived in barely three weeks ago, I got a lump in my throat. No present I ever received has been wrapped so sweetly; no gift was ever so precious.

July 20

Dear Jessie,

Tonight, we are in a hotel in Lima. The weather is cold and damp, just as it was when I came here three weeks ago. On Monday we will go to the American embassy to finalize your visa, and Peruvian immigration to apply for your Peruvian passport.

Our departure from Iquitos this morning was no less an adventure than the rest of this trip. I had called Aeroperu yesterday to confirm our reservations. They were sorry to say they had never heard of me before (although I held our plane tickets in my hand), and there were no available seats for many days. This is a genuine problem; there are only two ways in and out of Iquitos, air and water. Quique told me not to worry. I'd forgotten that, in his real world, he works as a labor lawyer, and not infrequently for Aeroperu.

All morning long, as I was gathering the last of our things together and making a "care package" of extra formula and diapers for families who may follow us in the *hostal*, the people here came to say good-bye. Together, they had bought a little painted wooden bird, and each of them had signed it for you. I have packed it with as much care as if it were family crystal.

When at last we arrived at the airport, many, many people were crowded together, apparently waiting for the same plane. Some had suitcases, others plastic bags, and at least one person was carrying some sort of bird in a cage—this flight will look like an airborne Third-World bus! Quique told me again not to worry and hustled us into a little sitting room. Waiting there was Alex, smiling broadly and waving an airline ticket in his hand; he has been hired by Quique and Charo to meet other families in Lima and bring them to Iquitos. Beside him were our old friends the court clerks and the *fiscal*, with their wives and children, bringing little gifts for you. We had said goodbye to Theresita at the *hostal*, and she sent word that she could not bear to come to the airport to say good-bye again.

After a little while, the flight was called over the loudspeaker, and all the people in the terminal rushed out across the runway with their luggage and *plásticos* and wildlife. Finally, Quique said it was time for us to go. The next few minutes are a blur to me of tear-streaked good-byes and concern for our luggage, but I knew when we got to the top of the airsteps that the passenger compartment of that plane would not seat another soul. Quique nodded then, and someone took me by the elbow and escorted us into the cockpit. Quique had remembered that I had been disappointed to have flown into Iquitos at night and so to have missed the view of the Amazon from the air. His farewell gift to us was the best seat in the house, a wooden crate in the cockpit.

And . . . what a gift! Though I had my doubts that the plane would ever get off the ground, when it did, the view was almost unbelievable. First, the amazing deep greenery of the rain forest and the twisting tributaries of the Amazon River, all cast against a turquoise blue sky. Then, going over the spectacular Andes, we remained at the same altitude while the ground, sometimes green and often snow covered, rose up to meet us. And as we finally descended, a cloud mass: the fog desert of Lima.

One day, dear child, we will go back again and see up close the parts of Peru I saw from the air today. One day we will go back to the jungle, to visit Maria and the *abuelita*, and to say thank you. In the meantime, whatever I have seen and heard and photographed I will give to you in whatever ways I can, so that you can know that the place you were born is a wonderful place and that coming for you was the greatest adventure of my life.

Being There

commentary

Jean and Jessie arrived home on July 28, 1990, Peruvian Independence Day. Jessie has grown fast; her two teeth are now joined by
a whole mouthful, and thanks to Jean and to a day care provider
who is a native of El Salvador, Jessie speaks Spanish as well as
English. She is a beautiful, active little girl.

I talked recently with Jean about her life back at home in the
United States. Being a single parent has been a challenge, but she
has no regrets. Life is richer—busier, but filled with more purpose.
Jean has a daughter to care for, but also maintains a connection to
Jessie's past. Unfortunately, she was unable to obtain a visa for
Theresita to come to the United States to help with Jessie and to
attend school, or even to arrange temporary visitors' permits for
Quique and Alex. But they write and send pictures and occasionally talk on the phone. Along with several adoptive families and
with the support of her church, she has gathered donations of
money to buy food and infant formula to send to Father J in
Iquitos and is lobbying to establish several self-help projects there.
"Since coming back home, I've been overwhelmed by how much
we take for granted and how easy it is to slip back into life and
forget what we left behind in Peru," she told me. "At least I can do

something . . . and maybe it will show that I haven't just taken my baby home to the United States and forgotten about how Jessie got here. My bond, and my commitment to Peru will last forever."

At the annual Peruvian adoptive families picnic that Jean attended so hopefully in the summer of 1990, over one hundred families now meet to relive their experiences in Peru and to see how each other's children have grown. Debbie and Terry, the couple who adopted their son Joey in Iquitos, have since returned to Peru to adopt a second child, as have other families. Jean, too, has started to think about expanding her family, but is hesitating. Since she adopted Jessie, Peru no longer officially permits independent adoption, so she knows she will not be able to adopt in the way she did in 1990. Certainly, a second adoption will take longer and will be more difficult; she is not assured she will be able to adopt an infant as young as Jessie was or have contact with her child's birthparent. Jean is now also far more aware, from reading and talking with other parents, of all the things that could have gone wrong; knowing about them means that another adoption will feel very different. "My time in Peru was really blissful," she told me. "Even the one thing that was really frightening for a time—the baby-selling accusations—was eventually resolved so well that I never considered it a threat again. I do feel I was blessed with good and honest friends in Iquitos, and I never felt any need to be suspicious of them or fearful of the government. I don't want that to change, but if I end up going back to Peru again, I know that just because I'm better informed, I'll probably feel a lot more cautious. And that seems like a real loss."

Despite her failed adoption attempts in Paraguay and struggles with her first adoption agency, Jean's eventual in-country adoption experience—an almost trouble-free three week stay—is extraordinary in light of international adoptions in general and Peruvian adoptions in particular. Some would not call it a "normal" experience. But what is normal? Preadoptive parents ask this question all the time, and agencies and parents alike are hard-pressed to give a solid answer. Unfortunately, experiences in the eighty countries worldwide and nineteen Latin American countries that Americans adopted from in 1993 vary too greatly to determine "normal." Is it Jean's three-week stay or a grueling twelve months, as cited by the

New York Times in a 1992 article? Is it traveling to meet your child and start the court process, putting him in foster care while you fly home and returning in four months when his adoption is complete? Is it meeting a baby in O'Hare Airport seven months after you first saw her picture, or is it traveling to Korea to pick her up only two months after hearing about her? In this unpredictable world of would-be parents and their would-be children, everyone from the U.S. State Department on down scrambles to keep up to date on current intercountry adoption policies and practices. Because the international scene changes so often and worldwide events impact directly on adoption, nothing is cast in stone. China used to take about five weeks, but it's now closed for the moment, one parent tells me. Russia is supposed to be closed, but the U.S. embassy is still processing visas for children traveling to the United States and warns adopters that an adoption can take an indefinite amount of time. During good years, Indian adoptees can reach their new homes in four months; but in 1992 fewer than usual children left India due in part to bureaucratic problems. South Korea hopes to phase out intercountry adoption by 1996, but adoptions are still going forward. Colombian and Philippine adoption programs continue to be well run, and many children are waiting there. One agency worker said she expected that Eastern Europe would be the "brave new world" of intercountry adoption. An adoptive parent who has done relief work in Asia thinks many more children will arrive here from Vietnam in the next few years. There is much speculation about future trends, but the information that prospective adopters want the most—how long will it take and how much should I expect to pay—changes yearly.

One "normal" factor in international adoption, unfortunately, is that adopters can expect to dig deep into their pockets. Even without complications or delays, adoption isn't cheap: parents can easily spend $12,000 to $15,000 and some adoptions cost far more. Adoption agencies require the first of a series of hefty payments as soon as a child is assigned; some may even require payment in one lump sum. If an adopter contracts with a foreign lawyer or other contact in an independent adoption, lump sums are often the case. "No wonder so many people find international adoption such a strain," says one father. "There are millions of children who need families but legal bottlenecks and crazy requirements create great frustration in terms of time and finances! I have a large income, luckily, but still this adoption was a serious financial burden. If it wasn't for my father actually giving me a large sum of money, we couldn't have done this. Half of that amount we spent, I'm convinced, was unnecessary."

The large costs involved and the time it takes to process adoption paperwork work against the child in all cases—and against the parents too. Jean was lucky that Jessie's adoption was completed so quickly, because parents who do stay longer often fall into a complex emotional as well as financial situation. The process of bonding with a new child starts very early, often as soon as a child's photo first reaches an adoptive parent, and certainly as soon as the parent takes custody of the child. Therefore, if things get complicated and parents stay longer than anticipated, they start feeling backed into a corner, completely in love with their new children but frantic over the time spent away from home and frightened that the long wait might mean that something is wrong and that the adoption will ultimately fail. Wading through a frustrating and unpredictable bureaucracy makes them furious over their situation—parents because of and in spite of the very country that seems to be holding them and their children hostage. With friends and family far away, most find it hard to keep things in perspective.

"Last night, Cristina pulled herself up to standing for the very first time," I wrote to my husband during a low moment in Peru. "It should be exciting, but instead I just got so upset, because all I could think of was how you're been cheated out of seeing it happen. When will the judge finally sign [the adoption decree]? Maybe never? I've been away forever and I'm feeling so frustrated and lonely. I miss Matt and I miss you and I wonder if I'll ever get home again." I read that while looking at Cristina, now safe at home and happily playing with her toys, and I know that all those moments of hopelessness were worth it. I don't know another adoptive parent who doesn't feel exactly the same way. But would we go through the same experience for the next child? If it were Jean's experience, I'd say yes in a minute. If it meant traveling twice to Colombia and living through a hotel bombing with a new baby; or, as two good friends did, staying almost a full year in Lima, Peru, while struggling with a corrupt lawyer, a coup, and the death of a mother back in the United States—no. Both of the families who lived through those incidents paid an emotional and financial price far beyond what they had bargained for.

No one should have to suffer through an intercountry adoption process. There is suffering enough—on the part of the birthparent who so regretfully relinquishes her child, of the child who leaves his genetic heritage behind, of the adoptive parents who often risk so much and whose intentions are so often misunderstood. And it seems from watching the intercountry adoption scene over the last five years that things are getting worse. So many countries that have welcomed adoptive parents in the past are in turmoil over the issue, and adoptive parents must stand helplessly by. "I'm sure there have been bad adoptions, and that's a real concern," writes a friend from Lima, Peru, "but I believe that the media blitz that would lead Peruvians to think that gringos are buying babies to use their body parts, or to keep them as slaves, is a smokescreen to divert attention away from the horrific real conditions throughout Peru, which cause thousands of underclass children to die of diarrhea, malnutrition, cholera, etc."

To set up roadblocks or to spread rumors or argue over the "right" of parents to adopt and give new life to desperate children who would languish in institutions or on the street anyway is completely counterproductive. It's become clear that a definite structure for the process of international adoption is needed before it disappears from sight. Significant new regulations exist in individual countries, but change is desperately needed at a higher level—because intercountry adoption is an international issue, caused by and affecting nations worldwide.

As a purely administrative issue, international adoption is a nightmare. Despite organized efforts that date back to 1971, there still exists no single legal or procedural approach to adoption—intercountry or domestic—that countries or even individual states within the United States have ever agreed upon. And because there seems to be no end in sight to the developed world's search for adoptive children and poor countries' supply of them, the need for cooperation to ensure legal, safe, and humane adoptions is essential. Hopefully, a solution is on the horizon.

The Hague Conference on Private International Law, a cooperative organization of mostly industrialized member states, has brought together developed and developing nations and more than a dozen international organizations to work on the issue of international adoption. Together, they have worked since 1990 to

formulate a multilateral treaty—The Hague Convention on Intercountry Adoption—that would

- establish safeguards to ensure that intercountry adoptions take place in the best interests of the child and with
  respect for his or her fundamental rights as recognized in
  international law;

- establish a system of cooperation among Contracting
  States to ensure that those safeguards are respected and
  thereby prevent the abduction, sale of, or traffic in children; and

- secure the recognition in Contracting States of adoptions
  made in accordance with the Convention. (Final Act,
  1993)

Not everyone is happy about this treaty, and there is much
speculation about how it will be implemented. Those who act
independently as adoption coordinators or adoption lawyers are
already worried about accreditation requirements after the treaty
is implemented in each country. People concerned with contact
between birthparents, children, and adoptive parents fear that the
treaty will either make it easier or more difficult to keep birth
connections intact. Everyone wonders if the structure for oversight
of adoption mandated by the treaty—"Central Authorities" to be
recognized or created in each country—will make intercountry
adoption more cumbersome and create more bureaucracy than is
necessary.

I asked Susan Freivalds, executive director for Adoptive Families
of America, about these uncertainties. "Of course there's fear of
change," she told me. "But I believe that some restrictions need to
be in place to make international adoption work for everybody.
What this is all about is creating a predictable process with oversight. And there's a lot to be said for predictability. Some people
have asked, `Why change anything? My adoption went fine.' Well,
yours may have, but others that started out exactly the same have
fallen by the wayside. Right now, too, if something goes wrong
there's often no place to complain to in many areas of the world.
The treaty will change that.

"The Hague Convention will legitimize intercountry adoption.
The reasons for adoption are clear in the treaty: it says right in the

Preamble that a child, `for the full and harmonious development of his or her personality, should grow up in a family environment' and that `intercountry adoption may offer the advantage of a permanent family to a child for whom a suitable family cannot be found in his or her State of origin.' Right now, adoption workers in other countries who work to provide for these children carry a great stigma. Not everybody approves of what you're doing when you escort an infant through the Seoul Airport and get on a plane to the United States. Now escorts and other workers will know that what they're doing has been internationally recognized as legitimate.

"I believe we'll have a period of turmoil as changes in intercountry adoption phase in. But there will be a long-term benefit to children worldwide."

The final Convention on International Cooperation and Protection of Children was completed in early 1993. After ratification by the thirty-six member nations and assent by nonmember countries, a standardized, international set of norms and procedures will finally be in place to guide countries in making the best possible decisions in establishing adoption policy.

The Hague Convention is good news—but for very few of the world's children. Jean and I and thousands of adoptive parents who traveled to our children's birth countries are only too aware of the endless numbers of children who will never be "rescued" by adoption, who are homeless or hungry or sick, who have nothing but dirty water to drink and who have never been immunized against disease. The United Nations Children's Fund tells us that forty thousand of them are destined to die each day because they don't get the very basics of care, and we know that but for the grace of God, the children we have adopted might have been among them.

Poor children and poor countries weren't always so poor. Years of struggle between East and West after the end of World War II and the recruitment of developing nations in that struggle depleted precious financial resources. The arms race funneled money into weapons systems instead of social programs, and economic and humanitarian aid for countries of the Third World was left far behind. Now, some of us are adopting children from the world's huge population of neglected peoples whose very circumstances are a result of our own country's past lack of involvement. Adoption is a very personal solution for very few of the world's poor, but it is a motivating force for those of us who have used it to form our families, and who might never have felt the personal connection to a poor nation that our adopted children bring with them. A growing number of adoptive families recognize a responsibility toward the countries that gave us our children; not just because of our own country's neglect, but in thanks for our sons and daughters. And there are many ways to fulfill that responsibility.

Besides educating our children about their native cultures and teaching them respect for their genetic heritage, we need to support and become active in relief organizations and self-help programs that work in developing countries, and encourage our children's awareness of this important work. We need to demand that our government become involved in basic, worldwide economic and social development programs that especially support women and children, the most powerless members of the world's poor population. In particular, we must demand that our congressional representatives support the United Nations Convention on the Rights of the Child, an agreement that ensures basic human rights for children of all countries; it is with great shame that I report that the United States has still not ratified this 1990 document. Similarly, when the U.S. Congress votes on implementing legislation for the Hague Convention in the next two years, we must demand support for it, too. Fundamentally, we must continue to learn about and insist on political decisions that better the very personal lives of all the world's children, and their families. Such decisions are not beyond our control; elected representatives are our direct link to Washington, and we must insist on their strong support for funding programs for children and families. Keeping up to date on these issues is essential, and for that reason belonging to an organization such as the Children's Defense Fund can keep you informed and educated on child welfare concerns.

If the world community works hard, things will begin to change: there will then be fewer families in desperate circumstances, and fewer children relinquished for adoption throughout the world. But what does that mean for people like me who are infertile, or people like Jean who don't have the option, for whatever reason, to conceive a child but still want to form a family? Will those of us who long to adopt see our options shrink further?

This doesn't appear likely. First, adoption in general will never disappear. There will always be circumstances that warrant the placement of some children outside their genetic families, and cultural acceptance of out-of-wedlock children will take many long years, especially in Asian countries. Second, our worldwide imbalance of rich and poor won't change overnight. Sadly, such political change is slow, and especially for poor countries, the social changes that follow are even slower. Outside intervention—foreign aid, CARE, the Peace Corps, other relief groups—will be around for a long while and so will intercountry adoption. As for the developed world's infertility problems, even though the medical technology that services the infertile population continues to grow and far more families are being helped, there will always be a population of infertile people who eventually seek to adopt.

Yet my inherent optimism in each nation's eventual ability to care for and accept its own children prompts me to look forward to a day when intercountry adoption is seen as an outmoded and unnecessary institution. Ironically enough, that's a possibility I hope for.

Lately, my daughter, who is now four, has been reading to her collection of stuffed animals. She gathers them together in her lap and opens up a picture book. "One day," she starts out, with a wise expression on her face. "Um, one day . . . " And then follows a jumble of words and phrases strung together from stories we've read to her at bedtime. One day, Cristina, I think. One day, how will your own adoption appear to you? I don't want it to be a jumble of words about world politics. We didn't start out that way; all we wanted was a daughter to love. But here we end, all mixed up in international relations, wondering about the fate of all the world's children instead of the one special little one we treasure. But finally, that feels right. Why should the stories of Cristina or Jessie end happily, and not those of the children who still struggle to stay alive in Iquitos or Calcutta or Bogotá or Seoul? Shouldn't each child end up as treasured and as safe and happy as our daughter is?

One day, maybe all of us together will find ways to make sure that all parents can comfortably plan and care for all our children. A family for each child, and a child for each family—now, that's a happy ending anyone could understand.

Postscript

"Tell me the story again, Mama . . . "

Once upon a time there was a woman who wanted very much to be a mother. She had many friends who loved her, but she was still very lonely because she had no child to share her life. So after waiting a long time, one day she called an adoption agency and told the person on the phone that she wanted to adopt the best baby in the whole world. "We have the best baby in the whole world," said the person on the phone, "but she's very far away. She's in a beautiful place in the rain forest, but it is very hard to get there."

"It doesn't matter," said the woman, who was suddenly very excited and afraid all at the same time. "If that is where the best baby in the whole world is, then I will go there."

So the woman who wanted to be a mother got on an airplane, and then on other airplanes, and after several days and nights of traveling, she came at last to the rain forest. And there, she met a lovely young woman who was holding in her arms a beautiful little brown baby in a pink dress. "This is my baby; I call her Topacio," said the young woman, whose name was Maria. "I love her very much but I can't take care of her, and no one in my family can help me. They tell me you can take care of her, and that you want very much to be a mother but have no baby of your own. So please," said Maria as she handed the baby to her, "make my baby your daughter." And they held each other for a long time, the lovely young woman and the woman who wanted to be a mother and the baby, and they cried together for sadness and joy.

And all that night, and for many days and nights to follow, the woman who had finally become a mother sat and stared at her beautiful new baby girl. She counted the baby's toes, and brushed her hair, and marveled that she already had two teeth (which the women in the town said was a sign that the baby was very advanced). She named the baby Jessie Victoria after her own grandmother, and Maria after the lovely young woman who had given her birth. The people in the hostal where they were staying called the baby Jesusita, which means "Little Jesus Girl."

And after several weeks, many papers were signed, and the baby's adoption was finally official. Then, it was time for the new mother and her baby Jessie to leave the rain forest, and Maria, and the *abuelita* who was Maria's grandmother, and all the friends they had made in Peru, to return to Chicago and begin their life there together. And although this was a very happy time, it was also a very sad one, and Jessie's new mother promised that one day she would bring her little girl back to visit everyone and to see the rain forest for herself.

And so they began the long journey from Peru to Chicago, with baby Jessie snuggled deep inside her new mother's front pack. Although there were many people on the airplanes and in the airports, and much commotion with all the suitcases and official papers, the baby slept peacefully for the whole trip. And then, just as the plane was landing in Chicago, Jessie woke up and began to smile and coo and kick her feet. And her mother knew that all the long years of waiting had been worth this one special moment.

And as they came slowly down the ramp from the plane to all their waiting family and friends, the new mother kissed her baby gently on the forehead and whispered softly, "Come on, Jess, we're finally home."

Jean and Jessie Knoll—home at last! *Photo by (Tia Felisa) Walden.*

Left to right: Katie Murphy, Cristina Lindsay, Peter Lindsay, and Matt Lindsay. *Photo by Stretch Tuemmler.*

Appendix

Resources

Each year, adoption resources grow by leaps and bounds; in our search for items to recommend, Jean and I constantly found even more to explore. To find what's best for you and your family, talk with other parents. Join Adoptive Families of America and read their publication *OURS*. Seek out adoptive family groups through adoption agencies or consider starting a group yourself. Discovering new resources is easier and more enjoyable within a group setting. And it's fun for your child!

Finding enough materials to learn more about our children's countries of origin can be frustrating. News coverage of the Latin American political scene can be confusing; things change fast and Latin American updates (like most news of the Third World) usually take a back seat to developments in Europe. Once in a while, in-depth news stories give a longer perspective, but they're usually few and far between. Be creative: Ask friends and families to keep an eye out for magazine and newspaper articles. Find out if the foreign language or political science departments of your local university offer public programs on international issues. Keep an ear tuned to public radio features on foreign affairs. If you are adopting in South America, look for copies of the *Miami Herald*, especially its Sunday edition. Because Miami is a major point of entry from South America to the United States, the *Herald* covers events in South America with a thoroughness unmatched by other English-language publications.

Consider developing a broader working knowledge of the country you will be visiting. Sorting through international politics is far less confusing after reading some history of your child's country of birth. For this search, you will probably find your local library to be a wonderful resource. Short histories contained in travel guides are just a start; you can use the library's *National Geographic Index* to locate articles that have been published in *National Geographic* about specific countries. Next, look for longer book-length histories either on your library's shelves or through interlibrary loan. Don't ignore the children's section of the library, either: in fact, the children's nonfiction collection may be the section to head for. Educational books and guides for school-aged children offer straightforward, general information that is easy to absorb—giving you a jump start on relearning about a part of the world you last studied in your high school civics class!

While in the children's section, take a look at the collection of folktales and picture books about Latin America and other foreign cultures (or once again, ask the librarian to find some for you through interlibrary loan). One of the joys of parenthood is discovering that the world of children's books belongs not just to your child but to you too. If you can increase your knowledge and appreciation of your child's cultural heritage at the same time, you have discovered a new and important resource.

Urge your library to purchase books that will increase its multicultural collection. This is a quiet, yet persuasive way of educating that benefits not just you and your family, but your community. As our families grow and change, so should our knowledge of the world outside the boundaries of our towns, cities, and country.

Organizations

Adoptive Families of America (AFA). 3333 Highway 100 North, Minneapolis, MN 55422. Probably the largest U.S. adoptive family network in existence. A nonprofit membership organization offering an excellent bimonthly member publication (see *OURS*, under Magazines), an annually updated adoption agency listing, information on how to start an adoptive parent support group, listings of adoption education and support groups nationwide, and information on adoption assistance benefits. Also offers free information that explains subsidies available to families adopting waiting children throughout the United States.

Children's Defense Fund. 122 C Street, NW, Washington, DC 20001. Provides education, advocacy, organizing, and lobbying around the issues of child welfare.

Committee for Single Adoptive Parents (CSAP). PO Box 15084, Chevy Chase, MD 20815. Provides information for U.S. and Canadian singles interested in adoption opportunities. Publishers of *Handbook for Single Adoptive Parents* (see Books).

International Alliance for Professional Accountability in Latin American Adoptions. PO Box 430, Shepherd, MI 48883. A professional organization dedicated to the advancement of ethical adoptions worldwide. Publisher of the newsletter *International Alliance Advocate* Further information on request.

International Concerns Committee for Children. 911 Cypress Drive, Boulder, CO 80303. This group keeps lists of organizations doing adoption placements.

Joint Council on International Children's Services from North America. PO Box 2880, Eugene, OR 97402. A coalition of adoption agencies, parent groups, and individuals working in the field of international adoption. Its activities include education (annual conference), advocacy, and promotion of child-centered practices through networking and information. Quarterly newsletter available.

Latin American Adoptive Families (LAAF). 40 Upland Road, Duxbury, MA 02332. A membership network serving the United States, but concentrated in the New England area. One branch in Ontario, Canada. Publishes *LAAF Quarterly*, a newsletter focusing on all aspects of the Latin American adoption experience, including updates on adoptive family gatherings. Member list of families published yearly.

Latin American Parents Association (LAPA). Current chapters: PO Box 4403, Silver Spring, MD 20914-4403 (Maryland); 55 Jeremiah Road, Sandy Hook, CT 06482 (Connecticut); PO Box

2013, Brick, NJ 08723 (New Jersey); PO Box 339, Brooklyn, NY 11234 (New York). LAPA is a volunteer association of adoptive parents committed to aiding persons seeking to adopt children from Latin America as well as assisting those who have already adopted. Another important goal is to improve the quality of life for children remaining in the orphanages of Latin America. LAPA accomplishes these goals by aggressively researching new sources of adoption in Latin America, supplying materials to orphanages, and providing education and social programs for its membership. NOTE: Local support organizations similar to LAPA and LAAF exist throughout North America. To find one near you, contact Adoptive Families of America (see above).

RESOLVE. 1310 Broadway, Somerville, MA 02144-1731. A national network of local chapters providing assistance to women and men dealing with fertility impairment and the professionals who work with them. RESOLVE offers education, referral, and support through both national and local newsletters; as well as information on all aspects of infertility succinctly outlined in excellent fact sheets. Most local chapters offer monthly meetings, groups, and symposia.

Books, Adult

Adoption: A Handful of Hope, by Suzanne Arms. Celestial Arts, Berkeley, CA, 1989. Complete rewrite and expansion of Arms's earlier *To Love and Let Go* (Knopf, New York, 1983). Stories about and commentary on the process of open adoption and its effect on all members of the adoption triad, especially birthparents. Although the domestic adoption situations highlighted are very different from those of intercountry adoption, the emotional content is the same. Especially important reading for understanding the feelings of birthparents.

Adopting after Infertility, by Patricia Irwin Johnston. Perspectives Press, Indianapolis, IN, 1992. This books makes an excellent bridge between the process and resolution of infertility and the decision to adopt.

Family Bonds: Adoption and the Politics of Parenting, by Elizabeth Bartholet. Houghton Mifflin, Boston, 1993. This is a book that will permanently change the way we view adoption. In the midst of so much current controversy about adoption, Bartholet offers a sound and critical analysis of options for infertile people and adopters. Using her own adoption story to illustrate her analysis of adoption policy and practice and current practices in infertility treatment, she makes a compelling case for revision of attitudes and laws that narrow the options for potential parents everywhere.

Are Those Kids Yours? by Cheri Register. Free Press, New York, 1991. Thoroughly researched and extremely readable, this book discusses all the issues you may expect to confront as a family raising children from another country. Fascinating reading.

Handbook for Single Adoptive Parents, compiled by the Committee for Single Adoptive Parents. Available through CSAP (see Organizations). This frequently updated guide outlines current adoption processes a single person might expect to experience and also devotes sections to the management of single parenthood. Includes anecdotal information about several special single parenting experiences, such as older child adoption or adopting a physically challenged child.

Raising Adopted Children, by Lois Ruskai Melina. Harper & Row, New York, 1986. Provides the adoptive parent with the best information available to date on family adoption issues, with a special chapter on transracial/cross-cultural adoption. A book you will consult again and again as your child grows. Highly recommended.

When Bad Things Happen to Good People, by Harold S. Kushner. Schocken Books, New York, 1981. Not a book about adoption, but a book to help understand and deal with unexpected devastation. If you've lost faith in the world and yourself, you will find compassion here.

I, Rigoberta Menchú, An Indian Woman in Guatemala, by Rigoberta Menchú, edited and introduced by Elisabeth Burgos-Debray. Verso, London, England, 1984. Winner of the 1993 Nobel Peace Prize, Rigoberta Menchú is a young Guatemalan peasant woman who has undertaken social and political activism in order to call attention to the plight of her people. The everyday life she describes of family and community mixes exploitation, horror, and injustice with ritual and beauty. It is an absorbing account of a culture forced to alter its age-old patterns in response to modern society's gross injustice and indifference. Though a story of Latin America, her story of an underclass with few options is similar to others worldwide.

Books, Children

Adoption Is for Always, by Linda Walvoord Girard. Albert Whitman, Morton Grove, IL, 1986. The story of Celia, who is frustrated and upset when she realizes for the first time what it means to be adopted. Slowly, she learns not only why her birthmother made an adoption plan for her, but also that her adoptive mother and father are for always. For children four and older.

Being Adopted, by Maxine B. Rosenberg. Lothrop, Lee & Shepard Books, New York, 1984. An excellent photographic essay with carefully chosen stories of three transracially adopted children, two from other countries. Especially suited for children seven and up.

The Day We Met You, by Phoebe Koehler, Bradbury Press (Macmillan Children's Book Group), New York, 1990. A read-aloud book for little ones explaining and celebrating a child's special "gotcha" or arrival day. Provides a perfect springboard for telling the story of your child's arrival. For preschoolers.

A Family in . . . series. Currently includes: Bolivia, Brazil, Chile, Peru, and others. Lerner Publications, Minneapolis, MN. These books follow the everyday activities of a typical family in each country. Beautiful color photographs, and a couple of pages of basic country facts, maps, and explanation of unfamiliar words used in the book. Although the text is geared toward children eight and up, younger children are sure to enjoy the pictures too.

The Family of Man, Simon and Schuster, New York, 1987. This well-known photographic portrayal of the world community was originally created by Edward Steichen for the Museum of Modern Art in New York in 1955. The newly revised edition updates the basic message of a universal kinship in all matters of life, death, family, grief, happiness, unity, conflict, fear, courage and the ultimate dignity of all humankind. This is a timeless and beautiful book. For all ages.

Horace, by Holly Keller, Greenwillow Books, New York, 1991. A gentle, funny book about differences. Horace is spotted and his parents are striped. Wouldn't it be great to live somewhere where everyone looked like him? He sets off to find out, and makes some comforting discoveries. A wonderful book for blended families! Ages three and older.

How It Feels to be Adopted, by Jill Krementz, Knopf, New York, 1982. A book of first-person narratives by mostly adolescent boys and girls, a mix of both domestic and some intercountry adoptees. For adults, a revealing look at what your child may be thinking about as she grows older. For children, a validation of all different feelings about adoption. For preteens and older.

Is That Your Sister? by Catherine and Sherry Bunin, Pantheon Books, New York, 1976. The story of a six-year-old's family, told in her own straightforward words. Catherine and her younger sister "don't have the same kind of skin or face or hair" as their parents or older brother. When other kids ask her about being adopted, she has lots of answers, and they're all in this delightful book! Ages four and up.

On the Day You Were Born, by Debra Frasier. Harcourt Brace Jovanovich, New York, 1991. A beautifully illustrated book that celebrates the natural world and its beauty and delivers the message that the birth of a child is always a miracle. All ages.

People, by Peter Spier. Doubleday, New York, 1980. A big book filled with detailed, whimsical illustrations showing how different people are throughout the world and how, ultimately, they are all the same. A really fun celebration of differences. Great for younger school children.

Susan and Gordon Adopt a Baby, by Judy Freudberg and Tony Geiss. Random House, New York, 1986. "Sesame Street"'s Big Bird reacts to the adoption of baby Miles with all the expected excitement and letdown an older sibling might feel. This gentle book is reassuring for an older brother or sister; but more importantly, it confirms for all children that adoption is simply another way for a child to enter a family.

What Color Are You? by Darwin Walton. Johnson, Chicago, 1973. A well-written social and scientific explanation of skin color that anticipates many questions youngsters may have and confirms each person's special place in the world, no matter what their appearance. For children nine and older.

Periodicals

Adopted Child. PO Box 9362, Moscow, ID 83843. Published monthly by Lois Melina, author of *Raising Adopted Children* and *Making Sense of Adoption.* A four-page newsletter that gives parents and professionals an in-depth look at a different aspect of adoption in each issue. Geared toward keeping the reader up to date on the latest in the world of adoption. Also available through *Adopted Child*: cassette tapes on subjects such as "Raising a Child of a Different Race or Ethnic Background," "Introduction to Adoption for Family and Friends," and so on.

OURS: The Magazine of Adoptive Families. AFA, Inc., 3333 Highway 100 North, Minneapolis, MN 55422. Published bimonthly by Adoptive Families of America, a national nonprofit adoptive parent support organization (see Organizations). OURS is packed with the latest information on adoption for members of all kinds of adoptive and prospective adoptive families. Many features and stories in each issue. Regular sections include a national listing of adoptive parent support groups; a selection of resource materials; a listing of parenting organizations; and a regular single-parent feature. Annual index and adoption agency update.

Travel Resources

Insight Guides, APA Guide Series, Prentice Hall, New York. Various publication dates. This excellent series of up-to-date travel guides goes well beyond the expected. Extremely well-researched chapters in each book educate the reader about the particular country's history, native cultures, and current political scene before moving on to descriptive travel information. Carefully produced maps, stunning photographs, and special sections on such varied topics as native music, wilderness trips, or a country's current literary life make each guide a valuable travel companion and keepsake. There are numerous *Insight Guides* in print for places as varied as Southeast Asia, Eastern Europe, Moscow, Peru, Korea, Chile, Mexico City, and many more.

Language Lessons. One of the most important things you can do to prepare for intercountry adoption is to make the effort to take language lessons of some sort, whether it be an intensive course at the local university or taped cassette lessons. As a guest in a foreign country, learning some of the language beforehand is a simple courtesy that we in the United States often ignore. Will it make a difference in the success of the adoption? Possibly.

Even knowing a small amount—a few key words and phrases—will show that you have respect and appreciation for the people you will be dealing with, which in turn will produce respect for you and an interest in your situation. Being able to be understood even a little will also go a long way toward helping you make a fast adjustment to life in a foreign country. Contact your local university for suggestions about classes or tutors (preferably, native speakers). A good language learning cassette series is put out by Educational Services Corporation, 1725 K Street NW, Washington, DC 20006.

United States Department of State Citizen's Emergency Center: 202-647-5225. Offers up-to-date travel advisories for specific countries, emergency help for U.S. citizens traveling in other countries, and other travel information and services. Have a pen and paper handy when you call.

United States Department of State Adoption Information: 202-647-3444. Updated information about intercountry adoption available by recorded message from the Office of Citizens' Consular Services of the United States Department of State.

Citizen's Consular Services, United States Department of State, Room 4811, Washington, DC 20520. Offers updated leaflets on intercountry adoption programs in many countries worldwide. Send a 9 x 12 stamped, self-addressed envelope and state the names of countries in which you have an interest.

Your State Public Health Service, Your State Capital or Centers for Disease Control and Prevention, Atlanta, GA: 404-639-1864 or 404-639-3311. To find out if you will need to take any health precautions or will require any immunizations for travel and long-term stay in a foreign country, contact the two services above. Your state's public health service will also be able to direct you to a local health provider for your immunizations and medications.

Your U.S. congressional representatives. Consider asking the offices of your U.S. senator or representative to issue you a letter of introduction. Such a letter, complete with seal and signature, can be an impressive and valuable document especially if you find yourself in a tight situation (as Jean did during her television interview in Iquitos). For telephone numbers and addresses of your senator or representative, contact your local library.

Miscellaneous

National Adoption Information Clearinghouse. 11426 Rockville Pike, Suite 410, Rockville, MD 20852: 301-231-6512, fax: 301-231-8527. Established by Congress and funded by the Department of Health and Human Services in order to provide easily accessible information on all aspects of infant and intercountry adoption and the adoption of children with special needs. Fact sheets (including one on intercountry adoption) and listings of adoption agencies, adoption triad support groups, and related experts in each state in the United States are available either free of charge or at a very modest fee. Computer searches on specific subjects, lists of films and videotapes on adoption also available.

Perspectives Press. PO Box 90318, Indianapolis, IN 46290. A specialty publisher offering books on infertility and adoption issues. Book list available on request. Enclose a stamped, self-addressed envelope for a copy of "Speaking Positively—An Information Sheet about Adoption Language." This is a discussion of correct vocabulary to use when talking about adoption.

Tapestry Books. PO Box 173, Ringoes, NJ 08551: 800-765-2367. A catalog of books about adoption, categorized by children's age groups and adult areas of interest such as open adoption, before you adopt, older child adoption, and so on.

Acknowledgments

Many generous parents, children, friends, adoption profession-als, and support organizations contributed to the making of this book. Though we cannot name each and every one, we grate-fully acknowledge all who lent their time, faith, and enthusiasm to our efforts. We would particularly like to thank those parents who consented to be interviewed for the Voices sections of the book; your stories are an inspiration to the adoptive families who will follow you. We also wish to thank the Chicago chapter of Single Adoptive Parents, RESOLVE of Maine, and our growing network of adoptive friends and their families. And without Amy Teschner of Chicago Review Press, this book would not be. Thank you.

To Rosario Gasquet we send a very special message of thanks and love. The scores of families you have helped to create are a permanent testimony to your commitment, dedication, and energy. We, our children, and the generations to follow thank you.

Index